Wisdom From the Trail

Inspirational Stories From Hiking

Wayne Sheridan
Keith Sheridan

Jeremiah 30:2 Publications

Wisdom from the Trail
Wayne Sheridan and Keith Sheridan

Copyright © 2018 Wayne Sheridan and Keith Sheridan

Jeremiah 30:2 Publications
Bristol, Virginia

Library of Congress Control Number: 2018904436
ISBN: 978-1-944187-28-6

All rights reserved, including the right to reproduce or store this book in whole or in portions in any form whatsoever without the permission of the publisher, except as provided by USA copyright law.

Unless otherwise indicated, all Scripture quotations are taken from the New American Standard Bible© (NASB), Copyright © 1960, 1962, 1963, 1968, 1971, 1973, 1975, 1977, 1995 by The Lockman Foundation. Used by permission. www.lockman.org

Scripture quotations marked (ESV) are from The Holy Bible, English Standard Version® (ESV®), copyright © 2001 by Crossway, a publishing ministry of Good News Publishers. Used by permission. All rights reserved.

Scripture quotations marked (TLB) are taken from The Living Bible copyright © 1971. Used by permission of Tyndale House Publishers, Inc., Carol Stream, Illinois 60188. All rights reserved.

Scripture quotations marked (KJV) are from The King James Version of the Bible.

All photos in this book are original to the authors and protected by copyright by Wayne Sheridan and Keith Sheridan.

Publication services provided by Christian Self-Publishing Association, https://www.christianwriterhelp.com/service/publishing-packages/

Printed in the United States of America.

ACKNOWLEDGMENTS

When I first gave thought to this book of inspirational stories from my hiking experiences, it was evident that my son Keith's experiences on the trail needed to be included. I am very thankful that he agreed, wrote his stories, and shared some of his photos. I am also very grateful that he was a very understanding fellow hiker when I was on the trail with him: going slower than his norm, allowing more frequent breaks, keeping up with the trail markers, and sharing words of encouragement.

It is always a challenge to minimize errata in a written work. Thanks to my wife, Alice, and a dear pastor friend, Herb Peak, pastor of First Christian Church, who edited this work in addition to the several times Keith and I made editing changes.

Thanks to my nephew, Jim Kochenburger, whose experience with self-publishing has been invaluable in the publication and marketing of *Wisdom from the Trail*.

Finally, thanks to my blog readers and Monday morning prayer group at Calvary Baptist Church in Bristol, Tennessee, with whom I tested some of the stories.

CONTENTS

1. WISDOM 1
2. INTRODUCTION 3
3. MORE THAN A TRACE 5
4. PREPARATION 9
5. USING THE MAP 13
6. GO LIGHT! 17
7. PERSPECTIVE 19
8. CALLING HOME 21
9. I WILL NOT GO THERE 25
10. MOUNTAINTOPS 29
11. VALLEYS 33
12. DISTRACTIONS 35
13. LOOK UP! OR LOOK DOWN? 39
14. SWITCHBACKS 41
15. THE PIT 45
16. FRIENDSHIPS 47
17. ENDURANCE 51
18. TIMES OF REFRESHING 53
19. EAT, DRINK AND BE HEALTHY 55

20. OVERCOMING FEARS. 59

21. KEEPING IN TOUCH 63

22. WHERE YOU BELONG! 67

23. DO WHAT YOU ARE MADE TO DO 69

24. FOXES AND MICE 71

25. THE BOULDER. 75

26. STORMS 79

27. WALKING IN THE CLOUDS 83

28. SNOW BLINDNESS 85

29. SEEING MORE CLEARLY 89

30. PUTTING ON ARMOR 93

31. THANKFUL FOR SMALL THINGS 95

32. ADVENTURE 99

33. TAKE THE NEXT STEP. 103

WISDOM

Does not wisdom call,
And understanding lift up her voice?
On top of the heights beside the way,
Where the paths meet, she takes her stand;
Beside the gates, at the opening to the city,
At the entrance of the doors she cries out:
"To you, O men, I call,
And my voice is to the sons of men.
O naive ones, understand prudence;
And, O fools, understand wisdom.
Listen, for I will speak noble things;
And the opening of my lips will reveal right things.
For my mouth will utter truth;
And wickedness is an abomination to my lips.
All the utterances of my mouth are in righteousness;
There is nothing crooked or perverted in them.
They are all straight forward to him who understands,
And right to those who find knowledge.
Take my instruction and not silver,
And knowledge rather than choicest gold,
For wisdom is better than jewels;
And all desirable things cannot compare with her."

(Proverbs 8:1-11)

INTRODUCTION

Hiking mountain trails is a joy and a challenge for me. Childhood asthma created the challenge, in that scars on my lungs reduce their efficiency. Getting enough breath is difficult, especially when climbing. Yet hiking is an important part of my life, and I have spent most of it taking hikes on mountain trails.

In youth, my family in Florida would travel Highway 441 north to the Smoky Mountains for vacation, where we would take day hikes in the mountains. Later, I learned of Jack Epps, a leader of Baptist work in Florida, who hiked many times on the Appalachian Trail. His enticing hiking adventures inspired me. Vietnam came next. Serving as a Navy corpsman with the 3rd Marine Division in the mountainous Quang Tri Province meant patrols on old trails and sometimes hewing new trails in the beautiful Vietnamese mountains. I thought I would have had enough mountain hiking after that experience, but the desire did not go away. Two active sons and a tomboy wife kept me hiking, usually in the Appalachian Mountains.

Hiking became serious for me after moving to Bristol, Tennessee, with the Appalachian Trail (AT) nearby. It began with a church friend taking overnight hikes on sections of the AT in the Grayson Highlands area not far from Bristol. Often Scott or Keith, my sons, would hike with me. While he was a student at Virginia Tech, Keith continued hiking in the Blacksburg, Virginia, area. He and friends from the university often chose the AT that travels through that region for their hikes.

One year I hiked with a group of men from a church in Lynchburg, Virginia, in the Sangre de Cristo Mountain Range in Colorado. We hiked from 9,000 feet up to about 11,000 feet, where we spent two nights in the thin air of an incredibly beautiful valley that featured fiery red blooms on Indian paintbrush plants; golden quaking aspens;

and a cold, clear creek winding through its middle. As beautiful as it was, the thin air and my restricted ability to absorb oxygen made the first day a struggle. After the first day, my lungs adjusted, and I could enjoy one of God's beautiful mountain gardens.

Keith graduated from college in 1998 and determined, after a lot of prayer and counsel, to hike the entire length of the AT from Maine to Georgia. Keeping in character, Keith researched the hike first and then made detailed plans. In June, 2001, Keith caught the bus from Bristol, Tennessee, for Maine. Catching a ride to Baxter State Park, he began a five-month adventure that started at the top of Mount Katahdin and ended on Springer Mountain, Georgia, in November. Oh, yes, you have to climb up Mount Katahdin's 5,267 feet to start the AT at its peak.

One thing Keith and I have experienced in common is that God has taught us spiritual truths consistent with the Bible while walking the trails. Neither Keith nor I are wise on our own. Any wisdom that is shared in these devotional stories is from God and the Bible. It is our hope that these lessons of wisdom gained on our hikes will be helpful to you as a reader on your trail of life. The inspirational stories in *Wisdom from the Trail* can be meaningful for devotional times, for encouragement, for wisdom, and for message illustrations. We pray that God will use these words to become living manna for each reader.

~Wayne Sheridan

MORE THAN A TRACE

Jeremiah 29:11 – *"For I know the plans I have for you," declares the Lord, "plans for welfare and not for calamity to give you a future and a hope."*

Early pioneers followed "traces" when searching out new lands. Buffalo, deer, and other animals created "traces" as they moved through the grasses or brush. A "trace" means a pattern of depressed or worn grass where animals like rabbits and deer frequently traveled. Traces were reliable since animals seemed to know how to get around barriers and where to go for water. Traces were not marked and could be hard to find. The pioneer learned to find them and use them to get where he needed to go.

As Native Americans and pioneers used the traces, they wore a path that became a trail. A "trail" is a cleared, often worn path through a forest, meadows, moors, or rough terrain. Sometimes great effort was put into forming trails, including creating markers to show the way. For instance, Daniel Boone took thirty men with him to develop the Wilderness Trail from Kingsport, Tennessee, across the Cumberland Gap to open up Kentucky for settlers.

The Appalachian Trail (AT) is a well-worn, marked trail that runs roughly 2,180 miles from Mount Katahdin, Maine, along the Appalachian Mountains to Springer Mountain, Georgia. It is of major benefit to both the day-hiker and the through-hiker who is traveling the whole trail. The great benefit of this trail is that others have gone before over the years to improve the trail and mark its way to some of the most beautiful views God has provided us on this earth. It is important to have trail markers, especially in snow or when a trail has been redirected. An attempt to hike the AT the whole distance without the markers would certainly lead to losing the way and an unsuccessful hike.

There are various ways a hiker can get help in staying on the desired trail. The AT is marked periodically with a white blaze to guide hikers in the right path. A change in direction is marked with two white blazes. There are books and maps for the AT that help a hiker know which way to go and how to get the most enjoyment out of the experience. It is helpful to hike trails with someone who has been there. After Keith hiked the whole AT, he and I went back to hike the 100 Mile Wilderness section. His previous experience was invaluable.

God has plans for each of us, plans that are for good. He has laid out the trail for us. Some of the trail will be difficult, even painful to traverse. Still, his trail for us is a good trail that leads to spiritual prosperity and to knowing him better. He has given us maps, experienced counsel, and markers to keep us moving on the right trail. The Bible is clear that God goes on the trail with us and will never leave us or forsake us (Deut. 31:6, 8). Our responsibility is to stay on the right trail by staying fit and by following helps he has provided. There are counterfeit trails (false religions and philosophies of men) and false counsel (lies versus truth) that could lead us astray from the right path.

One of my favorite hikes is from Carvers Gap, where Highway 143 crosses the Tennessee-North Carolina state line, north across the mile-high grassy balds to the Barn (an overnight shelter). The trail continues north over Big Hump Mountain and down to U.S. 19. One time Keith, a couple of his friends, and I were enjoying good fellowship on this section of trail on an alluringly gentle summer day. Our minds were on the conversation while we crossed Big Hump Mountain. The trail was following a forestry road down the mountain. That in itself was not a problem because the AT sometimes follows forestry roads or other paths, like the Creeper Trail in Virginia. It came to me that I had not seen a white slash for the AT for some time. I asked the others if they had seen one, and their response was, "No, we left that up to you." Oh, boy! I had grown careless with my responsibility for watching the markers to keep us on the trail. We were off the AT and had to retrace our steps back up the mountain until we found the place a double white slash had indicated a sharp turn in the trail.

The Bible is referred to at times as a "map for life" or the "manual for life," and it is of great benefit in staying on the right trail in life. The psalmist said, "Your word is a lamp to my feet and a light to my path" (Ps. 119:105). Daily explorations into the Bible, sometimes referred to as "devotions" or "quiet time" are helpful for the same purpose of keeping us focused on the right trail for living life well.

I have found that godly counsel from someone who has valuable experience on the trail of life helps keep me on the right path. Godly counsel in my life has come from my dad; my wife; my adult sons; pastors; and caring, experienced friends. Edifying books, videos, and songs can be a good source of godly counsel. I was impacted significantly by a songwriter who shared in a contemporary Christian song about his return to the faith of his youth. Beware of people who would pretend to have good counsel but do not have sound advice, advice that is usually half-truths or inconsistent with biblical truths.

A huge help for us in staying on the right trail of life is the Holy Spirit, who is at work in our lives as Christians. Jesus said, "But the Helper, the Holy Spirit, whom the Father will send in My name, He will teach you all things, and bring to your remembrance all that I said to you" (John 14:26). It has taken years for me to learn about the markers on the trail of life that the Holy Spirit gives. For example, he will make a scripture stand out for you that provides needed direction. He will give you unnatural peace in a decision so that you know it is pleasing to God. He will also disturb you when you are headed down the wrong path. The Holy Spirit is valuable to us moment by moment on the daily trail of life. His counsel can be accessed by prayer (not just talking to God, but listening as well).

Staying disciplined in watching for the markers of life, daily consulting the map of life, and seeking godly counsel as needed will keep you on the right trail of life. One day you may look back and see a life that was pleasing in God's eyes, a life of good and not evil, a life with hope and joy.

~Wayne

~Further reading – Ephesians 2:10; 2 Timothy 3:16; Jeremiah 29:11; 1 Corinthians 2:15; Proverbs 3:5-6. For further information about the Appalachian Trail go to the Appalachian Trail Conservancy at appalachiantrail.org

PREPARATION

2 Timothy 2:15 – *Be diligent to present yourself approved to God as a workman who does not need to be ashamed, accurately handling the word of truth.*

Walking up and down for ten to twelve miles on a mountain trail with a twenty-five pound back-pack is all I can handle in one day. When Keith was hiking the AT, he would put in days of over twenty miles. That meant he needed a lot of high-energy food and the right equipment to make it to the end. A short hike takes a little preparation. An overnight hike for ten or more miles takes more preparation. Keith prepared for a year for his five-month hike of over 2,000 miles from Maine to Georgia.

Keith, is good at preparation. He went about it like he was preparing for a final exam. Keith read about the AT and recommendations for those who want to hike it from one end to the other, a through-hiker. He talked with experienced AT hikers. He planned and purchased his clothing, footwear, and equipment. He evaluated his plan and made adjustments several times, always seeking to lighten the load. He planned his food—preparing boxes to be mailed by us, his parents, to general delivery locations in small towns at intervals along his journey. He planned for phone calls at intervals.

Keith took shorter hikes to get in shape and practice. He determined to go north to south, Maine to Georgia, and verified the best time of the year to start in frigid Maine. He studied his maps. To me, Keith seemed well prepared when he got on the bus in Bristol, Tennessee, and headed for Mount Katahdin in Baxter State Park, Maine, the head of the trail for a southbound through-hiker.

The trail of life is a long trail from our perspective, a short one from God's eternal perspective. Some say that the trail itself is preparation for us to go on the eternal trail in heaven. We are born with little preparation for life's trail on Earth. A baby starts with total dependence on others. Others teach us what they believe is truth so we will be prepared for life. Sometimes what people think is truth turns out to be faulty teaching. If we learn lies or partial truths, we can get off the right trail or be found lacking when the difficulties of the trail are upon us. It is important for us to learn truth from reliable sources. It is important, like Keith did with his planning, to evaluate what we think is truth and adjust to real truth when we find we have bought into a faulty idea. We need a reliable source of truth.

The Bible is God's instructions for taking our trail in this life. It is reliable truth to prepare us and guide us successfully along the trail. Paul wrote to young Timothy advising his disciple to study the Scriptures diligently, so he would not be ashamed in his handling of the truths found therein (2 Tim. 2:15). The Bible is a reliable, proven source of truth with which to compare other ideas from men. One person said that we either twist what the Bible says to fit what we want it to say (deceiving ourselves) or we correct our thoughts to conform to the truth of the Bible. Paul challenged the Roman Christians to "not be conformed to this world, but be transformed by the renewing of your mind" (Rom. 12:2). Truths found in the Bible help us transform our minds to what is truth.

Prayer is God's provision for communication with him. Unlike cell phones that have dead spots, prayer has no dead spots and can be used anytime, anyplace to reach the God of this universe. He is ready to answer. That's amazing! Someone said God's prayer provision beats the reliability, speed, and coverage of anybody's digital network. It is better than Wi-Fi. The only hindrances to prayer are those created by us. We either don't use it or we hinder it with unconfessed or persistent sin. God told Jeremiah, "Call to me and I will answer you, and will tell you great and mighty things, which you do not know" (Jer. 33:3). There are times when I have no answer for a difficult situation. It is wonderful to be able to call on the Lord who does have wisdom, resources, and interest for meeting us at the point of our need.

The church is like God's hiking club with experienced hikers to help give us good advice and encouragement for the trail. The Holy Spirit is our personal guide along the way. And just in case a crisis happens, the angels are our wilderness rescue squad. All this comes with the package of salvation in Jesus. That is, when we turn from clumsily trying to run our own lives and the sin weighing us down to forgiveness of sin and new life that comes with believing in Jesus; then God gives us a package that includes all these things plus an eternal relationship with him. It comes as a gift according to Romans 6:23. A gift for you and me already paid in full by Jesus when he died on the cross and was resurrected three days later.

It is not recommend for anyone to go far on the trail of life without taking the gift God offers now. You can get that gift by praying right now. Agree with God about falling short of his standards (sin). Ask God to apply to you the forgiveness paid for by Jesus on the cross. Ask him to come into your life to make you a new person with a new relationship with him as Lord of your life. If you know you have a relationship with God, but you are not enjoying all that comes with Jesus, then review what you believe against the source of truth, the Bible. Talk with God in prayer, asking him to show you—

through the Bible and the Holy Spirit—what changes are needed in your life so you can have all he has for you and be better prepared for the challenges that come your way on the trail.

~Wayne

~Further reading – Romans 3:23, 6:23, 10:9-10; the Gospel of John; *Mere Christianity* by C. S. Lewis

USING THE MAP

Psalm 119:9-11 – *How can a young man keep his way pure? By keeping it according to your word. With all my heart I have sought you; do not let me wander from your commandments. Your word I have treasured in my heart that I may not sin against you.*

Kilo Company was providing security for a small communications base on top of Hill 950 in Vietnam. I was senior corpsman for the company of Marines, and we were short of corpsmen at that time. Because of the shortage, I had to go on a perimeter day patrol with a squad of Marines. A couple of hours had gone by without incident. I did notice that the corporal who led the squad stopped frequently to check the map of the area. He and several other Marines in the squad were new guys to Vietnam.

One time he had three other men around him, and they seemed to be intensely discussing the map and looking around at the lay of the land. We were in an exposed position. Having learned to read maps in field-med school at Camp Pendleton, California, and having had a lot more experience doing so compared with the new guys, I moved up to the group and asked what they were doing. The corporal said he was not sure of our location and needed to know because he had to call in before returning to camp or the soldiers on guard might shoot at us.

The young corporal was wise enough to accept help. After looking at the map, I looked around at the hillside where we were standing and noted a steep cliff lying north northwest from the hillside on which we were stopped. I knew from experience that this would show up on the map as bunched-up contour lines, and pointed it out to the corporal. After he oriented himself, he called in our location and led us safely back to camp.

The Bible is like a map for the Christian's journey through life on Earth and preparation for eternity. Paul wrote to his young student, Timothy: "All scripture is inspired by God and profitable for teaching, for reproof, for correction, for training in righteousness" (2 Tim. 3:16). Psalm 119 is full of the psalmist's expressions of the importance of God's Word and his love for it. He made it clear in verses nine through eleven that being intimate with God through his Word is essential in living a life that is pleasing to God.

Paul also wrote to Timothy that he should study (the Word of God) to present himself without shame to God (2 Tim. 2:15). Like my experience in Vietnam with an enemy, there are spiritual enemies (Eph. 6:11-12) that would love to take advantage of us if we lose our way on the trail of life. Over the years, I have found various ways to study God's Word: (1) listening to teaching and preaching at Bible believing churches, (2) spending time in personal Bible study and prayer, (3) studying Bible verses more deeply by checking cross-referenced verses, using concordances for better understanding of particular words, and reading commentaries to see what trained theologians think about a section of Scripture, (4) meditating on specific verses to gain understanding for personal application, and (5) memorizing selected verses to be better prepared to personally apply a truth or to share a truth with someone else.

There are some principles that help in using the Bible as a map for life just like there are rules for using maps. One principle is that the Bible is truth and our lives need to line up with that truth as the final authority or standard for living. A second principle is that the verses of the Bible must agree with and support each other. This principle of agreement helps clarify verses that might seem to contradict other verses. A third principle is that the Holy Spirit is the Christian's teacher and he helps us understand and apply the Bible. (John 14:26). I like to ask God in prayer to teach me what he wants me to learn when I am reading in the Bible. When I struggle with the meaning of a verse or verses, I can ask the Holy Spirit to help me with understanding. It may take some time, but I find that understanding will come when I ask.

One day I was looking for my maps of the Tennessee/Virginia sections of the AT. I could not find them. I checked at a hiking store for new maps and found that the particular maps I like were not available. The older maps had a profile presentation of the trail that made it easier to see how steep a climb might be. The new maps did not have this feature. Thankfully, I later found my old maps.

Similarly, there are various versions of the Bible. Some Christians believe that only one version should be used. None of the more popular versions of the Bible are in the original language since we do not have the original documents. Some versions are easier for groups to read, especially people groups that do not read English. It is important to use a version that was carefully interpreted and compiled, one that you believe makes the truths of the Bible most understandable for you. Remember, it is the Holy Spirit who is ultimately our teacher. I have a Bible app on my smart-phone that allows me to compare several versions at one time on a given verse.

There are times when a particular scripture I was reading or studying stood out as a message just for me at just the right time. The Greek word for this is *"rhemah."* A *"rhemah"* is used by the Lord to encourage my discouraged feelings, direct my choices, correct my thinking, renew my faith, or move me from anxiety to peace. It seems that a *rhemah* comes more often when I am diligently seeking the Lord.

You can see that regular time spent in the Bible and growth in understanding its message is very important for staying on the right trail of life. If you have not been doing so, determine right now to set aside a time and place to regularly get with God and his Word. Paul gave Archippus great advice when he told him to just do it (Col. 4:17).

~Wayne

~Further reading – Psalm 119; Isaiah 55:11; *The Word of God with Power* by Jack Taylor

Note: There are several apps for phones, tablets, and computers that each provide access to various versions of the Bible and provide Bible-study tools and aids. I use Gateway and Blue Letter Bible. Just search for Bible apps.

GO LIGHT!

1 John 1:9 – *If we confess our sins, He is faithful and righteous to forgive us our sins and to cleanse us from all unrighteousness.*

Boots? Two weeks into his Maine-to-Georgia hike, Keith sent home a package containing several items, including his hiking boots. I was surprised to see such important gear come back to us. Later in a phone call home, Keith explained that he had bought hiking shoes that were lighter in weight than boots and that allowed his feet to breathe better. He noted that most through-hikers were using the lighter footwear.

Hikers tackling the 2,180 miles of the Appalachian Trail work at keeping the weight they are carrying as light as possible. That is why foods are often dehydrated and cookware is made of very light-weight materials. It is a priority for long-distance hiking. Some have been known to cut off loose threads to be sure they are carrying only what is required. Keeping the pack light on a several-day hike is essential for me. It improves my joy on the hike and my stamina for the distance, especially for climbing up a hill.

I find the same priority is true on the trail of life. I lighten the burdens by taking the Bible's advice to keep short accounts with God by confessing and repenting right away anything he reveals to me as a sin. How can I be forgiven for sin against the one and only holy, just God? Jesus, the Son of God who came to this earth on a redemptive mission, was totally righteous, making him the one and only acceptable sacrifice that satisfied God's requirement for death because of my sin and yours. I have been set free with forgiveness—the weight of guilt lifted. He not only has the authority to *forgive* my sin, but also the power to *cleanse* it from my life so it will not come back to be a burden again. This is available to all who believe in him.

When God reveals to me a wrong attitude, a harmful action I took, or a lie I have believed, it is a call to me to stop what I am doing and go to God in prayer. I confess my sin to him and receive the forgiveness and cleansing Jesus offers. I like getting relief right away! Letting sin continue to weigh me down is like carrying rocks in a backpack on the trail. It is harmful and foolish to do so when the solution to be rid of the weight is readily available through Jesus.

If you are carrying a burden, yours or someone else's, and that burden is hard to carry, go to God with it now. Confess to him (agree with him that it is sin) and picture in your mind laying it at his feet. He is able to handle those burdens, and the relief leaves you with more joy in life and in a better condition for facing the storms of life that will come along. Repeat as needed.

~Wayne

~Further reading – Psalm 32:1-5, Psalm 51:1-17, Psalm 55:22; Proverbs 28:13-14; Romans 6; *Traveling Light* by Max Lucado

PERSPECTIVE

Ephesians 2: - "...and raised us up with Him, and seated us with Him in the heavenly places in Christ Jesus."

One of the most beautiful sections on the AT takes the hiker north from Carvers Gap, part of Roan Mountain, along Grassy Ridge on the way to Highway 19. There are a series of mile-high mountain peaks with sparse vegetation and scarce weather-worn trees among the boulders and grass. It has not been determined scientifically what made or keeps these peaks bald. It is well worth the time to stop and take in the breath-taking views of mountain ranges standing tall across the horizon. I have hiked this stretch of the AT many times and never tire of its beauty.

From Grassy Ridge a hiker can see three or more states on a clear day. There are towns and roads that look like tiny toys. There are valleys with creeks or rivers racing through to the next valley and eventually the flat lands on the way to the ocean. I almost envy the hawks and crows that can see even more of God's beautiful creation from their lofty, soaring perspective.

One of the best known peaks is Grassy Ridge Bald, a 6,819-foot peak that can be reached by a short side trail off the AT. My wife, Alice, and I have hiked up and picnicked there after church on Sunday. I have taken friends up there to feast on the astounding views. Other times, I have gone there alone, just God and me working on my perspective.

It is not unusual for me to have one or more heavy weights on my mind and heart when I breathlessly work my way up to the boulder that marks the peak of Grassy Ridge Bald. I climb onto that boulder and search with my eyes Roan Mountain High Peak to the west. Then

I turn to soak in the view of mountain ranges as far as the eye can see. Every time, I am moved by their vastness, their stability, and their longevity. These mountains resist the winter storms and the frequent summer rain showers that work to tear them down. By comparison, Job said: "Remember that my life is but breath;" (Job 7:7), and that is how I feel when I see those mountains that were there long before I made the scene on this earth and will be there long after I exit. The perspective I gain seem to make the weights I hauled up the mountain grow less significant and lighter as I reluctantly head back to the valley.

"Perspective" is our point of view or outlook on something. When I am focused on my problems or someone else's problems, my perspective is limited and usually tends toward a negative attitude. Moving my view to a more lofty perspective, like choosing to hike to grassy balds, changes my focus and improves my attitude from negative to hopeful. Paul said the Christian's true perspective is from a heavenly viewpoint where we are seated with Christ above the circumstances. I remember the truth of who I am in Christ and what I have gained in him. My perspective changes so that I can see God's love, his goodness, and his sovereignty. I am reminded that he has a good purpose for my life even in the threats, storms, and suffering that come my way. Like the mountain ranges, I see how small my problems really are for God to handle.

If you are suffering and are focused on a problem, loss, or pain, try gaining a better perspective. You can climb the AT up to Grassy Ridge for a lofty view or you can pray and ask God to show you your problems from the heavenly place where you are seated with him.

Paul says if you focus on "whatever is true, whatever is honorable, whatever is right, whatever is pure, whatever is lovely, whatever is of good repute…, the God of peace will be with you" (Phil. 4:8-9)

~Wayne

~Further reading – Galatians 2:20; Psalm 73; *Sit, Walk, Stand* by Watchman Nee

CALLING HOME

Jeremiah 33:3 – Call to me and I will answer you, and I will tell you great and mighty things, which you do not know.

The last thing you want to hear while hiking on the AT above 5,000 feet high and miles from the nearest paved road is, "I'm having chest pains!" A group of men I know had hiked to the Barn in the Roan Mountain area one morning, ate a light lunch, and were headed back to Carvers Gap in the afternoon. The group had stretched out along the trail in twos and threes. My friend and I came up to a group of three, with one of them lying down on the up-side of the trail and another leaning over him. They immediately said, "He's having chest pains, and we aren't sure what to do." The man with the pain was awake and groaning off and on. Wiley Webb is a dear friend of mine.

His pulse was thready. I remembered the blood-thinning aspirin pills I always carry along just for this type of problem. Aspirin quickly thins the blood and might help increase the oxygen supply to the oxygen-deprived heart muscle. We got him to take the aspirin and drink water, lots of water. He had perspired profusely and was probably dehydrated. Dehydration is a serious problem for any hiker. We also turned to the only help we could reach. We prayed to God to help my friend with his need, to help us know what to do, and to help someone get through to 911. The man said that he thought he might have a nitroglycerin pill with him. He pulled out a small bottle. I had him take one right away and then another in about fifteen minutes. He finally began to get some relief.

While I was helping my hiking friend, others were trying to call 911, but no one could get a good signal, and we were unable to reach emergency help. Two men started back to the vehicle trying to reach

911 along the way. Two of us helped my friend begin taking short walks back toward the Barn where a vehicle could get to him when 911 was reached. We would go twenty or thirty yards and rest, then go again.

Eventually a signal was achieved, and the Carter County EMTs reached us by four-wheelers. He had begun feeling better by that time. The EMTs took him in a four-wheeler to a rescue vehicle and on to a hospital. It turned out he had experienced a mild heart attack. My friend is very grateful for all the help, but we all know it was the instant communications (prayer) with God and his availability, mercy, and grace that made the difference.

The ability to call home in prayer to the Lord at any time and any place without the problems of solar flares, no cell towers, or weak batteries is an amazing gift of God to his family. God is incredibly gracious to provide this kind of open communication with each of his children. Most of us cannot pull out our cell phone and talk with the president of the United States, the state governor, or even our mayor. I can't even reach my wife every time. The efficiency and reliability of God's prayer system puts the best cell phone networks to shame.

Keith called home every time he hiked off the AT to a town where there was a cell tower or pay phone. There were far too many times he was out of reach of any phone signal. Parents want to stay in contact with their children, no matter their age. God is like that. He wants to stay in contact with us all the time. Paul wrote: "Pray without ceasing" (1 Thess. 5:17). I picture praying without ceasing as being like walking with a dear friend somewhere and having a conversation along the way, some talking and some listening.

The reality is that prayer is an underutilized benefit of our saving relationship with Jesus. If you think your prayers are not getting through, consider that it will work much better when you gain by faith a believing relationship with God after he's made you his adopted child. It is very important to keep your sin account clean (1 John 1:9). Ask God to reveal to you any sin that might be hindering your prayer communication with him. Sometimes we do all the talking and do not listen, making it hard to catch his answer. He speaks to us through the Bible, the counsel of godly friends, and through "a still small voice" (1 Kings 19:12, KJV).

The one thing you need is to have the Lord's phone number. I like to say that his phone number is JER-33-3 for Jeremiah 33:3. You dial his number by "calling," and the connection is made with "faith." The word in this verse for "call" more likely means "cry out." Many times I have cried out to God about a decision I needed to make and I was clueless about the right way to go. Just like Jeremiah 33:3 says, the answers came, sometimes right away and sometimes later, but always just at the right time.

The Bible says in James 4:2, "You do not have because you do not ask." This may suggest a bigger problem. When we have an intimate relationship with God, it is normal to seek him in our times of need. When we have a lukewarm or cold relationship with God, our thoughts will more likely go to others or our own reasoning for answers. I find I get much better results by keeping a close relationship with the Lord.

Call home more often. Our prayers please the Lord; and when we are in need, no one has more resources or power with which to respond to our needs than God.

~Wayne

~Further reading – Ephesians 6:18, Hebrews 4:16; *Prayer: Life's Limitless Reach* by Jack Taylor; *How to Pray* by R. A. Torrey; *Prayer and Praying Men*; *Power Through Prayer*, and *Purpose in Prayer*, all three by E. M. Bounds

I WILL NOT GO THERE

1 Corinthians 9:26-27 - *Therefore I run in such a way, as not without aim;...but I discipline my body and make it my slave, so that, after I have preached to others, I myself will not be disqualified.*

One morning as my friend, Jeff, was driving the two of us along I-40 toward Davenport Gap, Tennessee, I looked up and saw a steep slope on the east side of the tallest mountain in the area. I commented to Jeff, "I'm glad I don't have to hike up that steep slope today." Jeff just grunted. His son was hiking north on the AT through the Smoky Mountains and we planned to hike in from the northeast to meet him at Cosby Shelter that evening. We reached the trail, put on our backpacks, and headed up the mountain.

About a hundred yards up the trail, I stopped, turned toward Jeff, and gasped, "I have to take a break, Jeff, but you can go ahead." Jeff gasped back, "I thought you would never stop!" Neither of us were in great trail shape. Childhood asthma had left me with less than normal ability to get oxygen from my lungs. So, it was not unusual for me on an uphill climb to go at a slow pace and take frequent breaks to catch my breath. I describe my breathing on uphill climbs as "sounding like a freight train."

I have been asked why I like to hike in the mountains with my limited breathing. At first, I accepted the difficulty as the price I had to pay to enjoy the incredible beauty of a wilderness trail over mountains. Over the years I have learned that the hikes remind me of my dependence on God, build humility, and grow determination. I gain in character and maturity because it is difficult. Paul's words about disciplining his body make a lot of sense to me. For you, it may be some other difficulty that God wants you to persevere through to obtain a prize in the end.

There is a method to my overcoming my difficulty. On a steep climb I have learned to focus on a root or rock several yards ahead and set it as a short-term goal. When I reach the goal, I push past it a few more yards before stopping. Eventually, I "go-stop-go" all the way to the top and to the rewards of getting there. Focusing on reaching one goal at a time and not the whole climb has given me the joy of hiking up some pretty tall mountains to some incredible views.

We climbed go-stop-go for more than five miles that day and achieved the top of the trail. We sat down for some lunch at the top. Jeff told me that we had just climbed over 2,000 feet in four miles up Mount Cammerer. I quickly looked up at him and gasped, "You're kidding me!" Mount Cammerer is that steep slope I had seen from I-40, the one I did not want to climb. It is a good thing Jeff did not tell me in the van that we would soon be climbing that steep slope or I might have said, "I will not go there; I'll just stay here with the van."

God has the ability to see down the corridor of time of our lives. He did not give us that ability. God in his intimate, complete understanding of the makeup of our lives knows that we would not handle well the foreknowledge of adversities, sufferings, and disappointments facing us in the future. He knows we might say, "I will not go there!" Out of his love for us God reveals just enough to get us where we need to go today. Jesus said, "So do not worry about tomorrow; for tomorrow will care for itself' (Matt. 6:34). If you want to live a relatively peaceful life that's pleasing to God and rewarding to you, work at trusting the Lord each step along the way and leave to him the unseen. Look for what God might be trying to teach you in the adversities along the way. Ask God for faith sufficient for today.

~Wayne

~Further reading - Proverbs 3:5-6; Philippians 4:6-9; 2 Corinthians 4:7-10

MOUNTAINTOPS

Proverbs 29:18 – *Where there is no vision, the people perish (KJV).*

The highest point in the state of Virginia, Mount Rogers, rises to 5,729 feet in the Grayson Highlands area. The AT winds its way around Mount Rogers. You can achieve the summit by taking the blue-blazed side trail from the AT to the top. Sometime before my through-hike on the AT, my family took the side trail to the summit. At the summit, there is a large boulder, some mossy ground, trees, and more trees. There was, disappointingly, absolutely no view of the horizon.

What makes or breaks a summit is the view. At the northern end of the AT in Maine is the glorious, domineering Mount Katahdin with its extensive views in all directions. The name is of Indian origin and means "greatest mountain." From where your feet are planted on the peak, the mile-high view miniaturizes forests, rivers, roads, and other mountains far away. I climbed to this peak in 2001 when I started a through-hike on the AT from Maine to Georgia. The view from the summit took my breath away.

At the southern end of the AT rests the humble Springer Mountain, more of a gentle hill, with a limited view to the south. It holds great value as either the beginning or the end of a great trek of more than 2,180 miles across many other mountains, yet its view gives little inspiration or vision.

Getting to the top of a mountain produces a great sense of achievement. My dad climbed up Mount Katahdin with me and a couple of my friends a few years after my through-hike. It was not easy for him to make the 10.4-mile round-trip hike to the peak and back. It had been a section goal of his to hike to the northern terminus of the AT at Mount Katahdin's summit. He was pretty tired when we arrived at the top, but he was blessed by the view and by knowing he had made it up a tough climb. Achieving difficult goals can satisfy the soul and build a "can-do" attitude when facing future tough goals. He faced prostate cancer a couple years later. The positive reinforcement of reaching hiking goals like the summit of Mount Katahdin helped see him through future tough situations like the battle with cancer.

Mountaintop experiences provide a different type of view, a vision. We reach mountaintops in our lives, and the experience can sometimes be tainted by the nudge in the back of our minds that this glorious time will not last forever; there will be a valley, or maybe even a swamp ahead on the trail. Sometimes our mountaintop experience can be obscured by competing issues of life that crowd out our vision. Should we lose our joy because of the "downs" of life, especially when they follow the "ups" of life? No. Should we lose our joy because of competing issues of this world? No. Paul shared in a number of his writings that he and other Christians still found their joy even in the midst of affliction (2 Cor. 7:4). Their joy was a fruit of the Holy Spirit. The young Christian church was set apart from the world by their joy even in their suffering.

How can the mountaintop experiences give us hope? Hope for me comes from remembering the views from the summits I have experienced. Soak up the views from the peaks in your life. Survey from where you have come. The vision from the top can give you hope that another peak is ahead when you are trudging through a valley. Remembering how God has shown his love for you and blessed you with his unfailing grace in past peak experiences gives hope in the darkness of the valleys where his sometimes unseen love and grace also abound. I often enjoyed a mountain peak because I could see the next mountain ahead on the trail and the one I had climbed previously. It gave me hope that I would reach the next peak based on my successful experience achieving the last peak. Success also involves vision-driven determination to slog my way through the swamps and valleys and persevere on the climb to the top.

Paul said in Philippians 4:8 to dwell on excellence and what is worthy of praise. Keep your focus on the upward goal of Christ when at the peak or in the valley.

~Keith

~Further reading - Deuteronomy 32:49; Isaiah 2:3; Micah 4:2; Matthew 17:18; Romans 15:13; Galatians 5:22

VALLEYS

Psalm 23:4 – *Even though I walk through the valley of the shadow of death, I fear no evil, for You are with me; Your rod and Your staff, they comfort me.*

Isaac Newton declared that "what goes up must come down." I have used the quote a number of times when climbing mountains to remind me that the trail will eventually change and begin to slope down to a valley. Mountaintops are inspirational, but valleys have their value as well. Sometimes "valley" is used as a metaphor for going through a difficult time, even the "shadow of death" according to the psalmist.

Others see a valley as where refreshing water is found, like a running creek. This is very important for hikers because water is not so available on top of the mountain and running water is safer than stagnant water. A valley may have more flora and fauna because of the water, and the shelter effect against winds and heat. In other words, a valley can be a source of refreshment for the weary hiker.

I remember seeing the Kidron Valley outside the wall of old Jerusalem where Jesus walked with his disciples on the way from the Upper Room to the Garden of Gethsemane on the rise of the Mount of Olives. The Garden of Gethsemane is where he would intensely pray about his upcoming death on the cross in payment for our sins. This is also where he would be betrayed by Judas and taken prisoner. Along the way, Jesus stopped in the valley where there was a grape orchard. He spoke his last teaching to his disciples before the cross. He taught about the vine (Jesus), the branches (believers) that produce fruit, and the husbandman (God the Father). That valley signified a place of fruit production. No wonder, valleys seem to have more towns and people than mountains.

This is pictured well by the Shenandoah Valley that stretches from the Potomac River in the north to the James River in the south through eight counties in Virginia and two counties in West Virginia. On its eastern side rise the Blue Ridge Mountains with the Skyland Drive and AT. These mountains are populated, but the Valley is far more populated and is a major agricultural valley in the eastern United States. This valley exemplifies a place for fruit production and growth.

When going through a troubled valley like a troubled relationship, serious illness, or crisis in belief, you will find the Lord is there. I like to picture God as a loving father who is sitting on his throne, and in my suffering I come to him, climb up into his lap and he puts his strong arms around me ministering love and security.

We do some of our best learning in the valleys. Affliction has a way of opening the ears of our hearts to the Lord's teaching. It is important to remember that while in the valley God has not left or forgotten you. He takes the trail with you leading you out of the valley in time. Seek God's benefits from your suffering; that is, learn from his teaching, bring glory to him as you trust in him during the suffering and develop a better understanding and concern for others when they are in a valley.

Mountaintops are glorious, but valleys are grand in their own way—a place of refreshing, fruit production, growth, and drawing closer to God.

~Wayne

~Further reading – John 15:1-11; *Secrets of the Vine* by Bruce Wilkinson; Hebrews 12

DISTRACTIONS

Psalm 73:1-3 – *Surely God is good to Israel, to those who are pure in heart! But as for me, my feet came close to stumbling, my steps had almost slipped. For I was envious of the arrogant as I saw the prosperity of the wicked.*

Bloodthirsty black flies, pesky mosquitoes, blisters, muscle cramps, equipment failure, tripping roots, and stumbling stones are some of the adversities my son Keith and I faced on the 100 Mile Wilderness trail in Maine. Focusing on any one of these adversities would have impeded the enjoyment of a beautiful, unique trail; the joy of hiking with my son; and the satisfaction of reaching the goal of completing the 100-mile trail. The most troubling adversity was equipment failure. The belt buckle on my new pack broke two days into the hike. A jury-rigged replacement buckle did not work as well as the original buckle and caused discomfort to the end of the hike.

We had progressed a little past sixty miles. The insect bites begged to be scratched, my left shoulder was hurting from the off-balanced pack, and energy was scarce. I focused on these afflictions and developed a complaining attitude. Keith noticed and stopped for a short break. He gently shared, "Dad, I have found that if I focus on the scenery and thoughts of good things, soon the hurting seems to go away or at least not bother me so much." He saw that I was listening and continued, "Focusing on the adversities could even create more difficulties because we try to compensate, and that can start other problems." I was surprised and pleased at his wisdom and decided to apply it. I started thanking God for the beauty around me and then started reciting scriptures that I had memorized. It worked! The bites, aches, and tiredness did not completely go away, but my new focus made it possible to better enjoy the day's journey and the rest of the hike. I think Keith also enjoyed not having to listen to my grumbling.

When we allow the adversities of life to get our focus off of Jesus and the important, good things of life he has given us, then the problems seem to grow larger and we move deeper into a negative attitude. It is important to prepare for these times by memorizing Scripture verses that will minister to us; by starting each day with prayer, seeking God to lead you along the way; and by staying in the company of fellow believers who will encourage you and speak truth to you in love when needed.

The psalmist Asaph when he almost stumbled and slipped says in Psalm 73 that it was when he entered the sanctuary (the presence of God) that he saw the truth about the end of the wicked. It changed his attitude to gratefulness for his relationship with God. When adversities are distracting you on the trail of life, go to the sanctuary and ask

Jesus to help keep your thoughts on things that are good, beautiful, praiseworthy, and excellent. Then follow Jesus as he leads you to a better attitude.

~Wayne

~Further reading – Philippians 4:6-9; Psalm 37; Psalm 73

LOOK UP! OR LOOK DOWN?

Proverbs 4:25-26 – *Let your eyes look directly ahead and let your gaze be fixed straight in front of you. Watch the path of your feet and all your ways will be established.*

Splat! I had been looking at the beautiful view near the top of Mount Katahdin on the AT when in the blink of an eye I was lying face down looking at the ground up close and personal. After I gingerly got up, checking to be sure nothing was broken or strained, I looked for the trip hazard I had obviously not seen. All I could find was a rock sticking up a little out of the ground. There are plenty of trip hazards on all the trails. If it's not a rock sticking up, it's a root or a large fallen branch. I think I have seen them all.

As Proverbs warns, it is important to pay attention to where your feet are going if you want to be secure. The wise man is referring to more than feet and walking. He is telling us to pay close attention to our pathway while walking the daily trail of life. The day is full of decisions: Do I walk with this person, in that direction, in this place, or in that environment? Do I submit my eyes to these temptations or my ears to those foul words? Do I say things or act in such a way as to bring glory to my Lord…or shame? The path of a Christian, or anyone for that matter, is important because it impacts our spiritual, moral, and physical health. Staying true to the trail God has called us to walk maximizes a useful, fruitful, and joyful life in God's kingdom. Paul said, "Therefore be careful how you walk, not as unwise men but as wise" (Eph. 5:15).

Looking down all the time is not required, or wise. If I hike a trail and look only at the trail immediately in front of me, I may miss out on the amazing views along the way and the animals that frequent the natural areas. Each trail presents special features of its own: boulders covered with moss, tunnels through thick growths of trees, caves, flowers, and berry-covered plants. I may also miss an important fork in the trail. It is equally important in life to lift your eyes, glancing around to regain your perspective, as it is to focus on the trail, watching the path of your feet.

The psalmist said, "Make glad the soul of Your servant, for to You, O Lord, I lift up my soul" (Ps. 86:4). Looking at the big picture can revive you. When focusing on the problems you or others carry, a look at the character and promises of God can lift your soul. When focusing on the regrets of the past or the threats of the future, a view of the love of God proved on the cross by Jesus can set you free. When wondering if God still loves you or cares because you have not heard from him for some time, revisiting the truths of the Bible or remembering his past, faithful, lovingkindness is encouraging.

Watching the path of your feet is important, but so is glancing up from time to time. A balanced, healthy life does both. It is best to discipline yourself to check out your path if you are usually looking at the world around you. It is best to discipline yourself to look up and glance around at the truth and the big picture if you tend to stay focused on the details. One of my pastors said, "It is best to glance at our problems and focus on the Problem Solver."

~Wayne

~Further reading - Psalm 37:23-31, 105:5; Hebrews 2:1

SWITCHBACKS

1 Corinthians 10:13 – *No temptation has overtaken you but such as is common to man; and God is faithful, who will not allow you to be tempted beyond what you are able, but with the temptation will provide the way of escape also, so that you will be able to endure it.*

Switchbacks are a hiker's friend. Some trails use them frequently and some sparingly. It seems that trails west of the Mississippi use them sparingly and those in the East use them more frequently. A switchback is where the trail changes direction, often 180 degrees, for a distance and then turns sharply back again. The purpose of the switchback is to make the trail easier in climbing or descending a steep incline or in going around an obstacle.

I remember camping with Alice, my wife, in Yosemite National Park when I was stationed in California with the military. We got up early on a cold, sunny morning and set out on a trail that would lead us to a high pond that was known as a beautiful scene with crystal clear water. After a couple hours of hiking up the trail using scarce switchbacks, I saw a path that had been worn in the woods by traffic. It rose steeply in the direction we were going. I told Alice that we should be near the pond and this would be a shortcut. She wasn't thrilled about it, but followed my lead.

After only a few yards climbing up that path, we stopped for breath. Climbing a steep trail without switchbacks is strenuous. She was less sure this was a good idea. I was too, but would not admit it.

I said: "Let's keep going. I think it's just a little ways up here." She reluctantly agreed, and off we went. The next time we stopped for breath, I told her to stay put and I would go a little further to check it out. I agreed that we would retrace our steps back to the main trail if it was not just ahead. A few yards farther up the shortcut the trail peaked, and there was a beautiful mountain snow pond. After deciding that I wasn't pulling her leg, Alice came on up to the beautiful view. In spite of how tired we were from going straight up with no switchbacks, we enjoyed seeing a beautiful, clear-water pond formed by melting snow.

We took the main trail and its switchbacks on the way back and were surprised by a view that overlooked a breathtaking canyon. If we had stuck to the shortcut without switchbacks to return to our tent, we would have missed the canyon view that was the highlight of that trail and we would have struggled to gain sure footing on the steep slope.

Switchbacks help in three ways. First, they make going up or down a steep slope easier. Second, changing direction gives you a different view so that you see more around you than you would from going in only one direction. Third, geographic conditions sometimes prohibit a trail around a mountain and switchbacks are used to climb above or below the obstacle.

God gives us switchbacks, changes in direction, on the trail of life. Sometimes we do not readily like the change; we even resist it. These changes are put in our trail of life because an all-seeing God sees down the trail and knows we either cannot endure the steep climb, need to change our focus, or have an obstacle that needs to be avoided. God is good and has good in mind for us. The changes he puts in our lives are for our good even if we cannot see the good right away. What God wants is for us to trust him, not choose our own shortcuts. The wise writer says in Proverbs 3:5-6, "Trust in the Lord with all your heart, and do not lean on your own understanding. In all your ways acknowledge Him, and He will make your paths straight."

I have grown to really appreciate switchbacks on the trail since I deal with restricted breathing. I am not so appreciative of changes in life, but I am learning to appreciate them better now that I understand more how God uses them. Try talking honestly to God about changes you confront. Tell him just how you feel about the change: joy or irritation. Be honest; he knows anyway and likes honesty. Then thank God by faith for the change, knowing he has good in mind for you. Ask God to show you anything that you need to know to encourage you or to help you in adjusting to the change. Repeat as needed.

~Wayne

~Further reading - Psalm 143:8; Genesis 37:3-35, 39, 50:15-20 (Joseph had a number of switchbacks in his life.)

THE PIT

Psalm 40:2 – *He brought me up out of the pit of destruction, out of the miry clay, and He set my feet upon a rock making my footsteps firm.*

It had been a long, hard day already when I came down the Mahoosic Arm in Maine, slipping and sliding on rain-wet rocks. It was more a stream than a trail. Bruised and soaked, I arrived at the bottom of the Arm facing a worse obstacle - the Mahoosic Notch.

The Notch is considered by many the most strenuous mile on the AT. Its near vertical walls have sent boulders tumbling down over the centuries to form a boulder field with only confined spaces to squeeze through, sometimes only as wide as a foot. And it was raining.

These are the times when you look for an escape. We send up prayers for a way out, a sudden resolution to our problems, or a sign from God to clear our confusion. Escape from difficulty is usually not God's way. Instead, we are often given the tools to walk the slippery path assigned to us by the trail maker. I am thankful that Jesus did not choose escape when he was facing the trail to the cross.

The Mahoosic Notch is a maze of boulders that confuse the hiker. Do I crawl through this possible dead-end hole under the boulder, or do I scramble over the slick rock to a dangerous drop on the other side? It is daunting, especially with the moistening mists that feed the slime growing on every surface. But there is help. Those who have gone before have painted arrows pointing the way, showing the route that will lead forward.

And so it is with our God. When he points us along a difficult path, he has gone before us and painted the arrows to lead us through it. Those arrows may be found in the Bible, in godly counsel, or sometimes in God's still, small voice. Our God has made the way for us. The question is whether we try to make our own way, follow a false guide, or follow the One who knows the way.

I came through the Notch safely, even carrying my pack the whole way. One time, I did slip and found myself hanging precariously by my fingertips clasping the edge of a rock. Hearing a subterranean stream slushing about underneath, I glanced down to see nothing but a black pit. Adrenaline surged, and in the next instant I was out of the hole and on my feet again.

In our darkest hour God will give us his power, his Spirit to guide and empower us. In those times it is no longer our strength that moves us, but the Lord's unlimited strength. We learn the most about our dependence on the Lord in those times. Those moments can bring us closest to him, fully depending on our Savior as he rescues us from the pit or carefully guides us through the maze.

~Keith

Further reading - Psalm 81:6; Ecclesiastes 3:10; Mark 14:36; Psalm 40

FRIENDSHIPS

John 7:33-34 - *Therefore Jesus said, "For a little while longer I am with you, then I go to Him who sent Me. You will seek Me, and will not find Me; and where I am, you cannot come."*

Although I started hiking the Appalachian Trail alone at its northern terminus, the peak of Mount Katahdin, I met many new friends along the way. Early on, I met two guys from Germany and a recently graduated high school student with the trail name "Slow Rider." In contrast to his trail name, Slow Rider liked to hike very fast.

A saying on the trail is, "Hike your own hike," which means if you need to take a side trail into town or hike at a different speed, then do it, even though your friends may make a different decision. This leads to your hiking friends drifting in and out of your life. After a couple weeks of hiking with Slow Rider he went ahead at a faster pace than I wanted and he stayed ahead the rest of the way.

Soon after that, I met a couple named "Peanut" and "Panama Red." It seemed that singles would often end up matched with a couple and hike together. Perhaps couples just need a friend to keep them balanced? I would stay with those two for many weeks until I went into a Vermont town and they kept going down the Trail. Many weeks later in North Carolina I would see Peanut and Panama Red again and finish the trail with them. In fact, I finished the trail with nine friends I had met along the way.

In life, friendships drift into and out of our lives for various reasons. The beauty of our Christian life is that each of these friends will meet up with us again in heaven.

With whom do we choose to hike in life? On the trail, I did not choose friends who could make me hike the fastest; rather, I chose friends who brightened the trail, made sharing the experience more fun, and caused my load to feel lighter.

One of those "friends" is my own dad. On September 11, 2001, my father planned to join me in the Shenandoah section of the AT. He had trouble getting to me when all transportation was stopped due to the tragic events that morning. His bus was stopped short of the rendezvous point for his ride, a friend, who would take him to meet up with me. That good friend drove the extra miles so Dad could join me on the trail. We hiked to a shelter and said that evening, "What better place to be than in the woods?" It was particularly quiet that night under the stars with no planes flying overhead.

We continued our hike because we did not want to yield to the terrorists' goal of interrupting our lives. We spent several days in the Shenandoah enjoying those peaceful hills while the world spun in turmoil outside our sanctuary. Although we did not set any hiking records, those days are some of our most cherished memories.

In life, our pride can make us want to choose the fastest friends, or those who can give us the best connections. The real, quality friendships, however, are those who can brighten our days, help us laugh, and lighten the loads we lift each day. And although God might call us away from our best friends at times, we always have a connection through God's Spirit in us and we look forward to a reunion of Christian friends in heaven.

There is a hymn entitled, "What a Friend We Have in Jesus." Jesus is the best, most reliable, and most loving friend anyone can have. If you do not know his loving friendship, then draw closer to him. Perhaps you have never truly received him into your life by grace through faith (see Eph.2:8-9). Why not do that now? Accept his invitation by prayer, letting Jesus know you believe in him and his forgiveness, and that you need him to be your friend.

~Keith

~Further reading - John 14:1-3; Ruth 1:16-17; Philippians 2:19-26; Proverbs 13:20; Luke 24:13-35

ENDURANCE

Hebrews 12:1 - *Therefore, since we have so great a cloud of witnesses surrounding us, let us also lay aside every encumbrance and the sin which so easily entangles us, and let us run with endurance the race that is set before us.*

Pain pulsed through my shins as I laid on my back, looking at the night stars and giving my dream to God. It was only a few days into my through-hike. I prayed, "God, if I am in this much pain in the morning, then my dream of hiking the Appalachian Trail (AT) will be over. Help me if you want me to continue." The next morning my legs were pain free, and I continued the trail. Five months later I finished the AT, by God's grace.

Many weights came against me, trying to keep me from reaching the end of the trail; such weights as painful backaches; sore, wet feet from slogging through bogs, fighting off clouds of mosquitos; trouble finding good water sources due to a shortage of rain in 2001; and encountering bears, rats, and porcupines. In spite of these weights I found hiking the trail was a joy. Looking back, I realize there were three factors in addition to calling upon God for help that turned the weights into joy.

First, I had people cheering me on. My parents, grandparents, and church friends were praying for me and tracking my progress. They seemed excited to hear my updates by phone when I could get to a nearby town. Knowing that they were pulling for my success kept me motivated. Everyone needs a support group.

Second, I traveled light. I cut out unnecessary items every chance I got, from trading in boots for lighter hiking shoes to cutting off unneeded pockets from my pack. Going light kept my spirit up and gave me extra energy and agility.

Third, I stayed flexible. I had pre-planned every step of the way, including how far to go each day and where to go off the trail to a store to re-stock food. There were times I chose to go off my plan. For example, one time I came across a ledge overlooking the Shenandoah Valley and abandoned my plans on hiking miles farther that day. The next morning I was awakened by a red-tailed hawk peering at me from his nearby perch, a blessing I would have missed had I not been flexible.

Are the pains of life getting you down? Look around you at family and friends that are praying for you and pulling for you. Do not be afraid to ask them to pray for you. Unload the burdens of unconfessed sin, worry, and anxiety. Give them to Jesus. Be flexible by listening to the Holy Spirit's guidance in your life and follow in obedience. Start experiencing the joy of the Lord and the ability to run the race with endurance.

~Keith

~Further reading - James 1:2-4; 1 Timothy 6:11-12; Proverbs 3:5-6

TIMES OF REFRESHING

Acts 3:19-20 - *Therefore repent and return, so that your sins may be wiped away, in order that times of refreshing may come from the presence of the Lord; and that He may send Jesus, the Christ appointed for you.*

A section of the AT aptly named the 100 Mile Wilderness stretches through the central area of Maine. The word *trail* is a euphemism for the pile of rocks, narrow boards, traversing bogs, and tangles of roots that are marked with white blazes as a pathway. The creators of that section of the AT struggled to stay off of paper-company land, and so had to go straight up and down mountains in the least horizontal and useful places possible. A hiker finds oneself wistfully looking across a flat tract of pines only to find the trail not designed for humans going straight up a rock or through a bog where God must have decided to store all of the world's extra mosquitos.

For three days I trekked along this landscape, always in perpetual motion trying to escape the foraging mosquitos. I ate meals standing up and pacing in a circle. Sleep was sporadic in a tent or mosquito net, hearing the little vampire bugs, each straining his proboscis trying to reach my skin. I readily sprayed the 100 percent DEET repellant into clouds of protection around me, except that the mosquitos of that wilderness treat DEET as a mere temporary obstacle between them and their feast.

And so, when my guidebook mentioned a mosquito-free camp not far off the trail, I glanced at the directions and quickly turned off on the one-mile trail down a muddy two-track road to a dock on a glassy lake. I found the boat horn and blew it once to shatter the silence of the lake. After waiting for five minutes, trying to fend off the mosquitos, a boat came to whisk me away to an imagined paradise across the lake.

We approached the bank, a manicured lawn upon which stood an American flag flying on a pole in a gentle breeze. Dragonflies and barn swallows dipped and weaved, happily making a meal of pesky bugs. I was able to sit on the porch swing and soak up the sunlight in relative peace. Several log cabins were teasing my hunger with the aromas of greasy burgers wafting across the manicured lawn. One cabin had burgers and cold drinks for sale. A few hours later, my belly filled with burgers, my bites soothed with balms, and my mind resting at peace rather than on edge in fight-or-flight mode, I made myself take the boat back to the dock to continue the trail.

That afternoon, I continued my fight against the bogs, roots, rocks, and bugs, but it was just a little easier. My time of refreshing had given me strength to make my way and a better attitude to help me enjoy some of the beauty and mystery of that wilderness.

On the trail of life we are constantly bombarded by stumbling blocks and surrounded by struggles that suck away our energy. The world begins to close in. It is not easy to find times of refreshing. It is important to purpose to set aside those times, knowing their importance for success in the rest of life. Jesus showed us in his time on earth how we should take times of refreshing. A time away to pray, to read the Scriptures, or even to take friends to the top of a mountain, were ways Jesus refreshed himself so he could do the ministry his Father sent him to do.

Jesus did not need to repent of any sin, but his followers are advised to find times of refreshing by repenting of bad attitudes, sinful acts, and false beliefs. To repent means to turn your heart and mind from something against God to God. Examine your life to see if some of your struggles, anxieties, or bad attitudes are caused by something that needs to be repented of and given over to Jesus so that you can enter a needed time of refreshing.

~Keith

~Further reading – Matthew 17:1-13; Psalm 23; Philippians 4:8-9

EAT, DRINK AND BE HEALTHY

Psalm 23:1-3 - *The Lord is my shepherd, I shall not want. He makes me lie down in green pastures; He leads me beside quiet waters. He restores my soul; He guides me in paths of righteousness for His name's sake.*

There is a sign at the beginning of the 100 Mile Wilderness section of the AT in Maine that says to carry in enough food for a hundred miles because there is no resupply along the way. Food for energy and water for rehydration are two essentials for long hikes.

How do you carry enough food for the energy required to climb mountains for the more than 2,000 miles of the AT? Keith had prepared boxes of dehydrated food for Alice and me to mail to him general delivery at certain towns. He would go off the trail to a nearby town's post office and pick up the package to resupply his food. There were baggies of rice, tuna fish packets, candy and energy bars, and packets of dehydrated fruits and nuts prepared ahead of time for shipment.

There are times hikers can eat well and times they have to go on less food. When in a town, it is normal for a through-hiker to eat a gallon of ice cream or several hamburgers in one sitting. Still, eating a lot of food at times does not prevent weight loss on a through-hike. When there are no towns, the ability to provide a lot of calories while keeping your carry-weight low is an important factor in food selection to pack.

The other essential is potable water, a supply of water that can be drunk without causing illness. There are chemical treatments that are very portable and easy to use for making water safe. Most hikers today carry water pumps with filter systems that remove the threatening bacteria, larger viruses, and amoeba. The really dangerous viruses are normally not found in water supplies in North America. There are usually sufficient streams or springs to resupply water daily. Without a sufficient supply of water, dehydration can occur that causes cramps; weakness; and, in severe cases, organ failure and death.

I find in my spiritual walk that feeding and watering are just as necessary as on a long hike. Selecting the right "food," the green pastures, is important to keep up my spiritual energy and to stay healthy. Paul said in Romans 12:2 to "not be conformed to this world, but be transformed by the renewing of your mind." If I feed my mind junk, like R rated movies or trashy TV, magazines, and books, I am more likely to lose spiritual energy and lower my spiritual immunity. If I feed my mind with the Word of God, I maintain more spiritual energy and health.

Meditating on God and praising him are like springs of fresh water. The Bible says that God inhabits his praises. When I praise the Lord in my quiet time or in public worship, I am refreshed and energized spiritually. Long periods without praise and mediation on the Lord and his Word weaken me and can ultimately lead to spiritual weariness and trouble that I never intended to happen.

Discipline yourself to plan for and implement times of taking in God's Word in private, small groups or in public preaching. Do the same by planning and participating in times of praise. I have found that with my cell phone and YouTube I can have choice praise music to enjoy during my quiet times. Find and protect your places and times to get into the Word, meditate on it, and enter into praise of the One who most deserves our praise. You will find your spiritual energy recharged and sufficient for the trail.

~Wayne

~Further reading – Psalm 119:9-16; Psalm 103

OVERCOMING FEARS

> Deuteronomy 31:8 - *The Lord is the one who goes ahead of you; He will be with you. He will not fail you or forsake you. Do not fear or be dismayed.*

Hiking in wilderness areas comes with some risk. It is not as high-risk as the inexperienced hiker might think. Still, most trails have potential for an encounter with a threat like a bear or a poisonous snake. When hiking in the Colorado Rockies I was impressed with the frequent posters warning about mountain lions. You might find a yellow jacket nest in the ground on the trail in late summer. Most shelters on the AT have mice or rats that like to come out during the night and forage for food. There are ticks, black flies, deer flies, and mosquitoes. Some people fear heights, and there are cliffs along most major trails through mountains. If that's not enough, my tendency to fear the dark tempted me with fear when spending nights on the trail.

It was essential to deal with fears in order to enjoy the hikes. I have found several truths helpful in dealing with fears:

1. **It is important to research the truth about what you fear.** Often our fears are overblown because of active imaginations when the reality about potential threats is not worth losing sleep over. If the threat is real and probable, it is important to know steps of prevention or to change the plans for the hike.
2. **God has given us a sound mind.** Use it to minimize risks. For example, experienced hikers know to hang food in a bag from a place where bears cannot get to it and to never eat food in your tent. I left food in a tent one time in Sequoia National Park. After a morning hike, we returned to find a small whole

in the tent and the food invaded, most likely by a squirrel. It only makes common sense to avoid bears with cubs regardless of how cute they may be. Black bears normally don't want to be around people unless provoked or unless they feel their cubs are threatened. But bears have learned that people have food especially in parks, so they may come around looking for a handout. Be sure you can see where you are stepping or reaching. Cover up, or use repellents for insects. It is usually better to travel with one or more fellow hikers. You can take practical steps like these to minimize risks on the trail. What are some preventive steps you can take to minimize risks to body, soul, and spirit on the trail of life?

3. **When you do not have control, trust in God, who is sovereign over all.** God keeps his word. Trust in his promises to go before you, be with you, and not forsake you. The Bible says that God never sleeps or slumbers. Philippians 4:6-7 tells us how to get peace and verses 8-9 tells us how to keep peace.

A funny story demonstrates these truths. I had taken a group of men, who were in the Haven of Rest's program for men with life-controlling problems, to the AT. We were on a hike to the Barn north of Roan Mountain. That evening I told the men that they needed to brush their teeth before going to sleep. I had learned this in Vietnam, having treated some men for rat bites on their lips. The rats could smell food and would check out the food odor in the men's mouths, sometimes with a nibble. Later that night I heard two men who had come from prison talking about rats. They had not brought anything with which to clean their teeth. These two men were big, tough guys, and I heard them say, "Do you think rats will really bite us while we sleep?" They talked themselves into fear that resulted in their moving their sleeping bags outside the shelter. They were not gone long. We overheard them complaining about the many daddy longlegs spiders that crawled over them when they stretched out on the ground. They said they would rather take a chance with the rats than to have those crawling bugs all over them. The program director and I had a great laugh over those guys.

These big, tough guys had made the threat bigger than it really was, because of their imaginations. Then they could have solved their fear just by brushing their teeth. Finally, they tried to deal with their fear on their own. How often do we exhibit the same pattern of behavior?

God is compassionate and dependable. The Bible says that he never fails us. He is a loving Father who cares for us better than any earthly father does. He has the capability and resources to do whatever is required for our benefit. Paul's letter to the Ephesians says that we have been adopted as children (Eph. 1:5). That means God values us as a father values his children.

God values us so much that he paid a very high price, his only Son, Jesus, who carried our sin to the cross and there paid the penalty of death for us so that we could be adopted and have a relationship with God like a father and child. That should give us a sense of security and peace in the Lord. Nothing will happen to us that God himself does not choose to happen for his purpose. Paul's letter to the Romans says that Jesus even defeated death itself. Our body will die, but our soul transitions to his presence. Is there really anything we need to fear other than being outside of God's protection?

Identify your fears. Apply the three truths about fear as often as needed. Walk your trails with joy and peace.

~Wayne

~Further reading - Psalm 27, Psalm 103:13; Ephesians 1:3-10; Philippians 4:6-9

KEEPING IN TOUCH

Philippians 4:6-7 – *Be anxious for nothing, but in everything by prayer and supplication with thanksgiving let your requests be made known to God. And the peace of God, which surpasses all comprehension, will guard your hearts and your minds in Christ Jesus.*

A lot of food is needed to keep a through-hiker going on the more than 2000-mile AT. A source of resupply is essential. On my through-hike on the AT in 2001, my parents periodically shipped packages of food, film, and other resources to general delivery in a predetermined small town along the AT. I would call my parents from the nearest pay phone when arriving at one of these small towns. I would update them on my progress and alert them about any additions or subtractions to the next shipment, including when to ship it. It was essential to connect with my source of resupply to be sure I had what was needed at the time it was needed.

Prayer can provide provision for the Christian. Someone said that prayer is faster and more reliable than anybody's phone or Wi-Fi. As we talk with God and request his help, he hears us and supplies at the right time our needs-physically, emotionally, and spiritually. Jeremiah 33:3 says, "Call to me and I will answer you, and I will tell you great and mighty things, which you do not know." What a great promise for us. Sometimes we impatiently feel that God is not quick enough, or does not give us what we want, but he is always faithful. His timing and his provision are perfect.

Sometimes I would call my parents after finishing a particularly challenging section of the Trail, such as the 100 Mile Wilderness, the Mahoosic Notch, or the Great Smoky Mountain National Park. It was rewarding to share my experiences, hear my parents celebrating with me, and hear their encouraging words spurring me to success.

God, the source of joy, loves to hear from us after our successes. He rejoices with us in them and he loves hearing us express our gratitude to him for his part in anything good that has happened. We are not able to succeed without his working in our lives, so he is deserving of our thankfulness. It is good to reflect on how he works in our lives and to share our joy with him.

During my hike on the Trail, my parents relocated to another house. When I stopped at a town to call them, their phone number no longer worked, and they could not reach me while on the trail! This was a little disconcerting in that I depended on them for my resupply. Later, I briefly joked that perhaps they found a way to finally be rid of me. I did find a way to get their new number. We reconnected, and they continued to faithfully send resupply packages and encourage me on my journey.

At times of silence from above, you may feel like God has moved away. You may feel abandoned by God. During these times, he is still faithful. He is covering us with his provision, even if we are unable to see what he has in store for us. Trust and keep walking the path set before you. Keep talking with him by prayer. He is listening. Maybe he is teaching you a character quality like patience. In time you will find evidence of his work in your life once again.

~Keith

~Further reading - Psalm 100; Isaiah 40:27-31; Matthew 7:7-11; John 15:5-11

WHERE YOU BELONG!

James 4:7 - *Submit therefore to God. Resist the devil and he will flee from you.*

One day while trekking along through the woods of northern Virginia in the Shenandoah National Park, I crossed paths with a large black bear that popped out on the trail as I was approaching. Having experienced a few black bears before, my instincts took over, and I yelled with a voice of authority, "Get off the Trail!" The bear must have been as shocked as I was at my own impertinence! To my relief, the bear quickly turned tail and moved off the trail and up a slope. The bear did not go too far up the slope before trying to hide behind one of the small, new-growth trees. He looked back my way. Thinking that I had better not linger, I quickened my pace along the trail and left the bear peering at me from behind his tree.

We all know that if he had wanted to, the bear could have torn me limb from limb. So how did I have any authority over the bear to tell him what to do? Similarly, when Satan pops out unexpectedly, crosses our path, and threatens to do us harm, what gives us any authority to tell him to go away? Like the bear, Satan is more powerful than us and can wreak havoc in our lives. Our authority comes from what Jesus did on our behalf on the cross and in the resurrection.

I believe the bear scampered from me because **I was where I belonged**—on the trail—while the bear was not where he belonged. The trail was my pathway through the woods, and all the rest of the woods belonged to the bear. Of course, my noisy yell helped too.

Any power we have to tell Satan to flee from us comes from the authority of Jesus who has already defeated Satan at the cross and with his resurrection. God has adopted us as his children, and he will fiercely defend his children when we run to him. We have been given authority to tell Satan to flee from us in Jesus' name. We are where we belong when we are close to God. Satan is not where he belongs when he harasses one of God's children. We are wise to avoid getting too close to him or in his habitat. Instead, we should follow the narrow path laid out for us by God's will where the Lord is and where, according to the psalmist, "You hem me in, behind and before, and lay your hand upon me" (Ps. 139:5, ESV). Then we can call upon the Lord, even cry out to the Lord (Jeremiah 33:3), to send Satan away when he is threatening us.

~Keith

~Further reading - Psalm 139; Ephesians 6:13-17; 2 Timothy 2:26; James 4:7; 1 Peter 5:8-9

DO WHAT YOU ARE MADE TO DO

Ephesians 2:10 – *For we are His workmanship, created in Christ Jesus for good works, which God prepared beforehand so that we would walk in them.*

Alice, my wife, and I had spent the night at the Barn, a two-story shelter that used to be a barn in North Carolina, just off the AT. It is near where the Overmountain Victory National Historic Trail crosses the AT. The Overmountain Trail was used by the Revolutionary War-era patriots to go south over the Great Smoky Mountains to fight a battle in South Carolina, The morning was cool and clear when we set out north on the AT. It is a moderate climb from the shelter to the top of Big Hump Mountain where we took a break. I took my pack off and plopped down on a large smooth rock that served as a bench. I looked around, taking in the beautiful day in the early summer. I was reminded of how this day was so unlike the harsh, bitterly cold, gale-force winds and heavy snow that have punished that mountain over many winters.

Standing alone a few yards away was a small, old evergreen tree that was sparse and wind-blown to one side from its battles with harsh winters. It was not as tall or full as the same type of trees lower on the mountain. Twisted limbs that leaned away from the prevailing wind told a story of its fight to hold on to the life it had been given in this place. Yet, as harsh as this place could be, that tree went on year after year just living the life it had been assigned.

I dropped my head down in prayer, asking God to forgive me for complaining about the relatively minor problems about which I occasionally mumbled. I noticed a tiny flower on a tiny plant growing in the place where the rock on which I sat met with some meager soil.

I thought, "How could a tiny plant like that survive in this harsh place?" It struck me that, like the tree, the plant was just doing what it had been designed to do. That little flower brought not only beauty to this harsh environment, but also hope that another plant would grow from it to be seen by someone else next year. That tiny plant was just doing what God had designed and assigned it to do. *Obedience* was the word!

While thinking on that little flower, a tiny insect came along and I went through the same thoughts about it. Whether a tree, tiny flower, or tiny insect, they all were living in obedience to their Creator who had designed and assigned them to live there in that harsh, beautiful place. They were just doing what they were made to do.

My prayer followed: "Lord, help me, like these, to live in obedience to you and to live in such a way as to bring glory to you, even in the hard times. Help me to be faithful and thrive in my place, time, and situations that you have designed and assigned me to live. Thank you for showing me these blessings today."

It is in the storms and struggles of life that our trusting in God makes us stand out, giving testimony to those watching us that our God lives and cares. He loves us and he is trustworthy. Ask God to help you live in obedience to him even in the storms and struggles so that you might be a testimony to encourage someone else and bring glory to your Creator.

~Wayne

~Further reading - Matthew 5:14-16; Luke 12:27; Psalm 1; Colossians 1:9-12

FOXES AND MICE

Song of Solomon 2:15 - *Catch the foxes for us, the little foxes that are ruining the vineyards, while our vineyards are in blossom.*

Shelters on the AT vary significantly, from enclosed structures in high-altitude, cold country to a two-story barn in North Carolina. Most are three-sided with a raised floor and a roof. The first time I laid my head down in one of these shelters, I noticed empty cans hanging on strings from the front rafter. The string was such that it would run through the middle of the can's bottom with a knot to hold the can about half way down the string. At the lower end of the string would be another knot tied midway on a three-inch stick. I asked someone about those odd things hanging around the shelter. The answer was important information for me to know.

Mice and rats have learned that shelters are a great source of food. Food left out by hikers, food spilled on the ground or shelter floor, and food in backpacks are their delight. They have to work harder at the backpack because they might have to chew a hole in it to get to the food—and they will do that. Their work is usually done at night while the hiker is sound asleep. Putting endangered food in a bag, like a plastic bag, and hanging the bag from the end of the string on the stick makes the food relatively safe because the mice and rats have trouble getting around the cans. Losing your food can be disastrous on a long hike. It is particularly frustrating to lose it to such a small thing.

King Solomon knew that the little foxes would eat the grapes. They can eat grapes and dig holes in the ground that interfere with good crop production. King Solomon was using that as an example of how little things can upset a relationship. The best way to deal with that is to prevent the little foxes or mice from doing their harm before they get started. Good relationships take work. Some of the work is to prevent big problems that can break up relationships (infidelity, abuse, unchecked anger, and selfishness) by taking actions that prevent little things from getting big.

The little things in a relationship can also be devastating over time, like water running over sandstone erodes it in time. Things like never saying, "I love you," or "I care about you"; never serving one another; never doing something nice that is unexpected; or living with poor personal hygiene—these can all tear down a relationship over time. Pay attention to the little things to prevent a big problem later.

One morning my wife was having struggling with her sinuses. She asked me a question before I headed out to work: "Why is it you stop and pray with other people when they have a need, but you don't stop and pray with me when I have a need?" *Ouch!* She was right, and it hit me between the eyes and in my heart. Thankfully, as poor as I can be with relationships, I did stop and pray with her right then. I have purposed to do more of that. I am grateful she communicated that unmet need with me so I could correct what seemed to me to be a little thing before it grew into a big thing.

Many years ago at a counseling seminar, Larry Crab made the case that the most important priority to God is "relationship." His case was that (1) God (the Trinity) is a perfect relationship, (2) the Ten Commandments in the Old Testament and the Great Commandments in the New Testament are all about relationship with him and with others, (3) God has purposed to build a family that will all be together in eternity, (4) the Great Commission in Matthew 28:18-20 is God's marching orders for the church to go and build up his family, and (5) the Bible says love supersedes faith and hope, and that God himself is love. Love is only experienced in relationship. This teaching caused me to put a higher priority on growing in relationship skills.

Think about the little things in your life that need attention. If you really want to improve, ask people around you, especially people in your immediate family, if there is some little thing you do, or do not do, that bothers them. Ask God to help you improve in that thing. Commit with God's help to work at improving your relationships.

~Wayne

~Further reading – Mathew 28:18-20; Mark 12:30-31; 1 Corinthians 13; *Improving Your Serve* by Charles Swindoll

THE BOULDER

Psalm 18:2 – *The Lord is my rock and my fortress and my deliverer, my God, my rock, in whom I take refuge; my shield and horn of my salvation, my stronghold.*

A favorite and frequented section of the AT for me is the trail between Carvers Gap and Highway 19. It has such beautiful high-elevation views. The Barn, standing a little over five miles north from Carvers Gap, is a great place to spend the afternoon and night. The hike to the Barn and back to Carvers Gap is a little more than ten miles. I also like to hike to the Barn, spend the night and continue the next day over Little Hump and Big Hump mountains to Highway 19 for a total of fourteen miles.

The trail going north up to Grassy Ridge Bald from Carvers Gap gets moderately steep with a lot of rocks. Just before reaching the fork where the AT turns left around Grassy Ridge Bald, the trail comes upon a huge boulder. I rarely go past that boulder without stopping to stand or sit on it and rest after dealing with the rocky trail. It is a great place to contemplate God as my rock.

The psalmist describes God as his rock at least twenty-five times. I cannot believe that the shepherd boy anointed king was referring to a rock that can be held in your hand and skipped across the water. David did use a smooth stone from a brook to bring down Goliath. So, do not count out the power of even a small rock. I believe David in his psalms was referring to a boulder. He saw and probably stood on, sat on, and hid behind plenty of boulders as a shepherd boy in the boulder-strewn area of Israel.

That boulder on the trail to Grassy Ridge is big enough and stable enough to always be counted on to be there. It is big enough to sit on when I need to catch my breath, and it provides me a great perspective of the area around. That boulder could be hidden behind if I needed refuge from the gale force winds that can blow at the mile-high altitude.

That's the way God is—always dependable and faithful, mighty enough to provide refuge from any storm, and a source of rest when the hiker on the trail of life is weary. Jesus said, "Come to me, all who are weary and heavy-laden, and I will give you rest" (Matt. 11:28). The way to benefit from God the rock is by trusting him to always be there, to love you always, to have good in mind toward you, and to never forsake you. Read his Word and follow his instructions. Take your anxieties and troubles to him in prayer, then watch for God to respond. Continue to obey any instruction he may give you or any truth he brings to memory. Like David, God will be your rock.

You cannot have much of a relationship with a boulder, but through Jesus' death on the cross and his resurrection, he gave you access to God. You can have a personal relationship with God, the Rock, now. "If you confess with your mouth Jesus as Lord, and believe in your heart that God raised him from the dead, you will be saved" (Rom. 10:9). Do not hesitate to rest on the Rock. If you do not have a personal relationship with God, turn to him and ask him into your life to forgive you of sin and to be your rock, your boulder. "And it shall be that everyone who calls on the name of the LORD will be saved" (Acts 2:21).

~Wayne

~Further reading – Psalm 27:5; Psalm 31:2-3; Psalm 62:2, 6-7; Proverbs 3:5-6; Philippians 4: 6-9

STORMS

Matthew 8:24-25 – *And behold, there arose a great storm on the sea, so that the boat was being covered with the waves; but Jesus Himself was asleep. And they came to Him and woke Him, saying, "Save us, Lord; we are perishing!"*

Alice, Keith, and I had driven to the top of 6,288-foot Mount Washington, in the Presidential Range of mountains in New Hampshire. We could not resist taking a short hike from the peak of Mount Washington on the Appalachian Trail to the neighboring peak and a little beyond. It was refreshingly cool, and the view was breathtaking. Included in the view was a small area of dark clouds that was growing and seemed to be coming right at us.

We turned back toward the pavilion on Mount Washington and stepped rapidly, wanting to get back before a lightning storm hit. We didn't make it. The dark clouds poured rain mixed with hail on us. The worst thing was that lightning punctuated with loud thunder was all around us. Urgently we bent over and tried to speed on to get away from the lightning. At first, the urgency of our situation kept us from noticing that we had become wet and shiveringly cold. It was terrifying. We began to feel the cold.

An SUV was coming up the access road to the pavilion. Our hope that they would see us and stop was rewarded. They slowed down and then stopped. We were so relieved to be in that SUV, and even more so to soon be inside the safe, warm pavilion. That little adventure cost me a new, dry sweatshirt for wet, chilled Alice.

Keith and I have been caught in several other adventurous, dangerous storms on the mountains. It is part of taking trails of any length. The trail of life has its own storms, and they can be very severe. Sometimes you can see them coming, and other times they come upon you unexpectedly. If you have the right equipment, apply wisdom, and get the right help, you can get through the storms on the mountain trails and on the trail of life.

The right equipment for hiking includes a rain jacket with hood, a pack cover, dry clothing, and dry matches. I like to keep a little dry kindling in my pack. It is important in a place where you can get we and chilled by wind to try to stay dry or to have the ability to get dry and warm to avoid life-threatening hypothermia (body temperature that is too low). If you get chilled, build a fire to help you get dry and warm.

Wisdom on the trail first says to avoid a lightning storm. But if you are caught in one, you do not want to be at the highest point in the area. Try to find a shelter where you are not exposed so readily to lightning. If no such opportunity exists, get as low to the ground as you can. When you can, start working on getting dryer and warmer to avoid hypothermia. Wisdom also says to seek help when you need it and not to be so proud that you reject it when it's offered. It is wise to hike in groups of two or more, especially on the more treacherous sections.

Equipping ourselves for storms in life includes having a war chest of memorized scriptures, an active prayer life, a church family, and well-exercised faith. The Lord is always trustworthy and says, "I will never desert you, nor will I ever forsake you" (Heb. 13:5). Another way to equip yourself for storms is to be sure your spiritual armor is on and in good shape, as described in Ephesians, chapter six.

Wisdom for dealing with storms in life includes avoiding choices that lead to unnecessary storms, looking for God's purpose in the storms and applying the truths you have learned to the situation. Jesus was not caught off guard by the storm on the sea. He said the problem that was causing anxiety for the disciples was their weak faith. It is likely that their faith grew that day from their experience in the storm with Jesus.

Apply faith (unconditional trust in the Lord) during your storms. If your faith is weak, call out to Jesus like the disciples did when they had lost hope. Jesus is the right help in the storms of life. Your storms are not an accident. God uses the storms to teach us and we do some of our best learning in the midst of storms of life. Ask God to show and teach you what he wants you to learn. Then be sure to watch, listen, and be a willing participant when he starts revealing the lesson to be learned.

As I go through storms of life, I have learned to be better-equipped for the future storms. I have added to my treasure chest of biblical wisdom, and my faith has grown stronger each time. Now it is a joy to help others see these truths about dealing with the imminent storms of life. God will use your lessons learned to help others like your spouse, children, grandchildren, neighbors, fellow workers, and fellow church members. Are you well-equipped, have a treasure chest of biblical wisdom, and have a strong faith? Let God build these in your life through the storms. You may find that God uses what he has built up in your life to help someone else make it through the storms along the trail.

~Wayne

~Further reading - Ephesians 6:10-18; Psalm 27:5, 32:7, 37:39, 46:1, 50:15, 86:7, 107; Nahum 1:7; *Victory in Spiritual Warfare: Outfitting Yourself for the Battle* by Tony Evans

WALKING IN THE CLOUDS

Habakkuk 2: – *And the Lord said to me, "Write my answer on a billboard, large and clear, so that anyone can read it at a glance and rush to tell the others"* (TLB).

Four of us traveled toward Elk Park, North Carolina, watching the raindrops steadily fall on the SUV's windshield. We planned to hike from Elk Park, which forms a pass between White Top Mountain and Mount Rogers, the highest peak in Virginia. When we arrived at Elk Park, the rain was easing and low-lying clouds engulfed us. Someone mentioned that at least it would be cooler hiking and the clouds should burn off with the rising sun. The group enthusiastically set out north-bound on the AT, winding up and around Mount Rogers toward Wilburn Ridge a few miles away.

It was our plan to eat lunch at Wilburn Ridge around noon before backtracking to Elk Park. Wilburn Ridge is about one mile beyond the turnoff for the side trail that leads to the tree-covered peak of Mount Rogers. We reached the turnoff for Mount Rogers and soon arrived at the junction of the AT, a horse trail, and the trail to Grayson Highlands State Park parking lot. Wilburn Ridge should have been in view, but we could not see it. The clouds had lingered and obscured the view all around. We all asked, "Which way do we go?"

What happened next reminded me of what God has done many times before when one of his children needs to know which way to go but cannot due to doubts, fears, self-interests, and lack of a close relationship with the Lord, sometimes called losing "your first love" (see Rev. 2:4). There can be interference from the shouts of the world, abiding sin, and disabling insecurity. What happened next was started by a simple prayer: "Lord, help us know which way to go."

I saw the clouds begin to thin out enough to see a nearby mountain, but not Wilburn Ridge. I looked around and just saw clouds. The clouds cleared in another direction. I faintly saw something protruding through the clouds. The cloud cleared and there it was, Wilburn Ridge, as clear as a billboard. That deserved another simple prayer: "Thank you, Lord!" We took the trail to the right, climbed to the top of Wilburn Ridge, and enjoyed lunch while sitting on boulders in the company of one of the wild horses who inhabit that area. The presence of her colt provided an extra treat.

I have often had to pray that prayer, "Help me, Lord, know which way to go," in a decision of life. God wants us to know his will. Jeremiah wrote this prayer instruction from God: "Call to Me and I will answer you, and I will tell you great and mighty things, which you do not know" (Jer. 33:3). Another meaning for the Hebrew word interpreted *call* is "cry out." It is not unusual for me to not have a clue about what to do. So I cry out to God for him to show me "great and mighty things" that I "do not know." When you have prayed, begin looking for the cloudiness to clear.

If you can identify clouds, such as an abiding sins, that are keeping you from seeing clearly, or if you have grown cold or even lukewarm in your relationship with God, then confess it and agree with the Lord on the right way for you to go. Then set out on the right trail. You can pray expecting him to respond in his timing. But you must be willing to wait and then travel the way he shows you, even if it is not what you expected. Because God is good, loving, and just, you can trust him with the way you should go. There is no better way to hike the trail of life than with the clarity God provides.

~Wayne

~Further reading - Psalm 40:11-13, 139:23-24; Proverbs 3:5-6, 4:20-27; 1 John 1:8-9

SNOW BLINDNESS

Proverbs 14:12 - *There is a way which seems right to a man, but its end is the way to death.*

Snow blindness usually refers to the blinding light from sunshine reflecting so brightly off pure white snow that our eyes cannot see clearly. There is another type of snow blindness that occurs when a layer of freshly fallen snow keeps a hiker from clearly identifying the trail. This happened to me and a small group of men on the Brumley Gap Trail in southwest Virginia.

The pure white of freshly fallen snow is beautiful. The psalmist says, "Wash me and I shall be white as snow," in referring to God's ability to cleanse us spiritually. So when I see fresh snow, it reminds me I was forgiven by God through Jesus and that forgiveness came with cleansing so effective that the metaphor "white as snow" applies. That is a pleasant reminder. Snow is not always so pleasant.

One time I was in the lead for a small group taking a day hike on the Brumley Gap Trail near Abingdon, Virginia. It was during the transition from winter to spring. The trail is higher along Brumley Mountain's ridge. It is a moderately difficult trail that connects Laurel Lake with a group of boulders called "the channels." Snow had fallen the day before our hike and we did not expect any difficulty from it since it had already melted where we started the hike.

A short climb on the trail to the ridge of the mountain was enough for us to experience a lower temperature and snow covering the ground. During one stretch of the trail, the ridge narrowed and was covered with a grove of small trees and snow. I looked for the trail mark on a tree or big rock and, regrettably, I saw none.

No leader wants to admit that he has lost the trail. I had to stop the group and tell them to stay put while I searched for the trail. After fighting through the barriers of tree branches, I finally identified a clearing through the trees that was the trail. The men did not let me forget my error. It was a humbling experience.

How had I lost my way? There were scant white slashes on trees because there were only a few trees large enough to be marked. Then the usual clarity of the trail was blurred by the destruction of winter. Finally, the dependable clarity of the path caused by the wear of many feet was obscured by the white layer of snow. It struck me that my problem with losing the trail was like spiritually getting off the right path due to something that seems beautiful at the time but later blinds the Christian to the truth.

There have been times along my trail of life that I have been so sure of myself in terms of doing "good" for God or others that I strayed from the path God wanted me to take. It's easy to take a path that seems right at first but later leads to unproductiveness in the kingdom. The culprit is often *self-righteousness*—a condition that sneaks up on Christians like that snow crept up on me. It can blind us from the truth that we are a people who need God's constant input into our lives to stay on the right path.

Christians who have been on the trail longer seem to be more susceptible to this problem. Sometimes I get so used to the trail that I stop checking for trail signs. That's when I get lost and have to backtrack. It's important to keep reminding ourselves that we are dependent on God's directions in our lives every day. The cure for self-righteousness is to humbly agree with God about it, to grieve over our sin, and, when we stray, backtrack to the basic disciplines of a godly man.

Basic disciplines of the Christian life include getting in the Bible regularly, praying often (prayer includes listening, not just talking), serving others, giving as God leads, and disciplining the body and mind (e.g., fasting). The Holy Spirit in us will keep us on the right trail when we walk in these basic Christian disciplines. I call it "doing required maintenance."

~Wayne

~Further reading - 2 Timothy 3:16; Jeremiah 33:3; Galatians 5:13-26; 2 Corinthians 9:6-8; Romans 12:1-2

SEEING MORE CLEARLY

Ephesians 1:18 – *I pray that the eyes of your heart may be enlightened, so that you will know what is the hope of His calling, what are the riches of the glory of His inheritance in the saints.*

Trails that traverse the higher peaks can provide a unique opportunity to see more clearly in the purer air, both on the horizon and in the night sky. One enjoyable experience from being on a mountaintop at night is seeing the way stars stand out in a clear sky. They are more visible because they are not hidden by competing man-made lights and low-level air pollution. The Bible's use of the term "stars beyond count" becomes real when you see a clear view of the heavens from high up. Constellations stand out more clearly.

One time I was hiking with several other men at about 11,000 feet in the Sangre de Cristo Range in Colorado. The first night the sky was clear of any clouds. We stood on a rock outcrop and looked up at the uncountable stars. At that elevation, pollutants, moisture, and other molecules are much less densely packed, making the heavenly lights shine through much more intensely. I have often heard people talk of vividly seeing the Milky Way, our galaxy. I had never been able to identify it. That night at 11,000 feet I saw our home galaxy so clearly that it was evident why it is called "milky." It was beautiful, massive, and so milky with so many heavenly bodies.

How often have I heard Christians confess that they have difficulty knowing God's will for themselves? It sounds like my difficulty seeing the Milky Way. I have found that when I remove the obscuring pollution of sin and blinding competition from daily living life, I can see and know God's will and his ways much more clearly.

Another time when desperately needing to draw close to the Lord, I found that a quiet devotional time with just him and me was very important. It helped me to see and know God more clearly. It is best achieved by having a specific time and place, a time and place set aside just for a private meeting with God. For me that was very early in the morning. It also meant a place without competing demands, sights and sounds that would distract me and obscure the Word. For me that place is my basement office. There I can freely pray, read, play music and sing, shout, and ponder without bothering others or their interfering with my time with God.

Another help in hearing more clearly from God is to keep short sin accounts. That means if you or I become aware of sin (selfish attitudes, harmful practices, or wrong beliefs that are contrary to God's ways) we agree with God about that sin (confess) and ask him to help us choose him and his ways over that wrong way in the future (repentance). This may require you to take steps to cooperate with the Holy Spirit in changing you. For example, if you are having inappropriate sensual thoughts, you may have to quit watching a TV program or certain movies, or visiting certain computer sites. Paul gave the following advice in Philippians 4:8-9: "Finally, brethren, whatever is true, whatever is honorable, whatever is right, whatever is pure, whatever is lovely, whatever is of good repute, if there is any excellence and if anything worthy of praise, dwell on these things." It may require forgiveness previously withheld, or seeking forgiveness.

Jesus provided all that is needed to be forgiven and to be set free from the power of sin. Be grateful for that fact and put this truth to work. Some call confession and repentance of sin spiritual breathing. Confession is exhaling to remove spiritual pollution in our lives (1 John 1:9), and inhaling is asking God to fill you with his Spirit. Examine your life to see if you have spiritual pollution or competition from the world that is obscuring your ability to know God and his will. Then spiritually breathe. You may be amazed as this new freedom from inhibiting sin allows the Holy Spirit to do the work God has planned for you and through you.

Since it is the Holy Spirit who knows the mind of God, it is important to give him freedom to work in your life and to listen to him. You will find that the Holy Spirit uses the Bible, counsel of godly people, circumstances, and an internal peace to speak to you. Counsel of people, circumstances, and peace should be considered when they line up with the Bible. The Holy Spirit will never lead you contrary to truth as revealed in the Bible. Finally, be sure to follow the Holy Spirit's lead with obedience.

My prayer is that God may bless you with enlightened spiritual eyes so that you may know the knowledge of the hope of his calling and the riches of the glory of his inheritance in the saints (Eph. 1:18).

~Wayne

~Further reading - Psalm 119:105, 130; Proverbs 3:5-6; Romans 8:6, 26-28; Romans 12:2; Colossians 3:2

PUTTING ON ARMOR

Ephesians 6:13 – *Wherefore take unto you the whole armor of God, that ye may be able to withstand in the evil day, and having done all, to stand* (KJV).

It was a very hot day when I crossed the Blue Mountain Ridge. It is significant in that it had been devastated by the zinc-smelting industry at the town of Palmerton, Pennsylvania. The ridge itself is like a desert. All of its foliage is dead, trees are strewn all over the dry ground, and the springs of water are poisoned. I was out of water!

Continuing on and parched, I reached Lehigh Gap, scrambled down, and found a beautiful spring on the far side, including what looked like chilled cans of soda pop. I would have gladly filled my water bottles and nursed my thirst on tasty beverages, except that I noticed just in time that the spring was surrounded by a swarm of hornets. Hornet stings are the worst. It was torture to be so thirsty and so close to an unreachable source of quenching my thirst and not be able to reach it.

At first, I threw rocks. Hornets are very good at dodging rocks. I realized this was a poor strategy and that it was just making the hornets angry at me. Sometimes I try to meet my own needs this way: I use the wrong strategy to grab at what I feel I need. However, God knows how to fulfill my needs much more appropriately, and in his perfect timing. Have you noticed that God often makes us wait for what we think we need right now? I think sometimes he waits to act for me to stop floundering around and "throwing rocks" so that I will get desperate enough to look to him alone.

Satan also likes for us to struggle in our own strength. He will tempt us and frustrate us while dangling what we think we need in front of our noses. How do we respond? Paul told the Ephesians to put on the "whole armor of God" in order to benefit from God's strength and mighty power. He has us clothe ourselves with truth, righteousness, peace, faith, salvation, and the very Word of God. When we don such defenses, Satan is powerless to get us to eat that proverbial "apple."

Despite sweltering from a hot day, it came to me that I should clothe myself in my rain shell. I wore a long pair of pants, my rain jacket, and a mosquito net over my head. Adequately defended, I was able to march up to the spring—only to find that the delicious cans of soda pop were empty, and likely the reason the hornets were jealously swarming the spring. But God knew that what I really needed after a dehydrating day was thirst-quenching water from a cool mountain spring.

This is so like human nature, to struggle for what we think we need, fighting and fuming for our desires. However, once we give in, give up, and release ourselves to the will of God, he gives us not what we so desire, but what we really need. God defends us, replenishes us, and heals us. His solutions are always so much more satisfying and rewarding than what we thought we needed. The Lord keeps us from temptation and from the evil one.

~Keith

~Further reading - Ephesians 6:10-18; John 14:6; Hebrews 10:10, 14; John 14:27; Galatians 2:20; 1 Corinthians 9:25; Hebrews 4:12

THANKFUL FOR SMALL THINGS

Revelation 7:12 – "...saying, 'Amen, blessing, and glory, and wisdom, and thanksgiving, and honor, and power, and might, be to our God forever and ever. Amen.'"

A favorite section of the AT is where it heads north from Carvers Gap. My wife and I were hiking it one day along Grassy Ridge to see if we could gather some of the wild blueberries that grow along the trail. The berries are small but very tasty. If a hiker can get to them before the deer, the berries are a tasty treat along the trail.

On another day, hiking along the same trail, we were treated to the bright oranges, reds, and yellows of flaming azaleas in full bloom. There are rhododendron that bloom along this same trail at a slightly different time. It is so easy to be grateful to the Creator for these small, spirit-lifting treats.

Beyond Grassy Ridge Bald at a certain time of the summer are beautiful red blooms on a lily named Gray's Lily. These lilies are found in that area only and seeing them bloom is a special joy. On down the trail, the AT travels along the North Carolina-Tennessee border. Along the sides of the trail grow very small plants, about 1-2 inches high, with a small number of dark green leaves. While hiking this stretch of the trail, I have picked a couple of these leaves and chewed on them, enjoying the refreshing taste of teaberry in my mouth.

Eventually, the trail winds around and generally down to a hollow where the Barn sits. The Barn is a two-story barn that was converted to a shelter. The view makes it a special place to stay, and there is always space at that shelter.

Past the Barn the trail journeys across Little Hump and Big Hump mountains. Keith and I have eaten mouthwatering wild strawberries on Big Hump Mountain. Sometimes along this section of the trail long-horned cattle that graze the mountain in summer are within sight. Amazing—some of those horns are at least six feet across!

Keith was in the New Jersey portion of the AT on his through-hike in 2002. It was hot, dry, and dusty. Water sources usually available were dried up. Occasionally he would come to a shelter in which someone from the area had left bottles of water or other drinks. Those who leave these treats are called "trail angels" by the hikers, who are very grateful for the acts of kindness that make their trail much more enjoyable.

I am always grateful for an unexpected or especially good water source, a flat section of trail, switchbacks, little irises with blue flowers, a moss-covered boulder, dry firewood, no biting insects, blooming wildflowers, a cloud to give a break from the hot sun, a ray of sun breaking through the clouds on a chilly day, a gentle breeze, and a breath-taking view. I am also grateful that God helps me see the amazing creativity and diversity, beauty, intricate and exacting design, power, and durability of his creation.

It seems that these special treats are so much more noticeable when on hiking trails. Crowds, concrete, stress, urgency, and noises inhibit our appreciation for the small things all around us that are worthy of our appreciation along the daily trail of life. Things like a smile, a laugh, a child's giggle, a silent moment, a fresh aroma, a tasty meal, someone waiting for us when we get home, a warm hand, words of encouragement, shelter from the storm, and a quiet moment with the Lord and his Word in the morning are examples of things that deserve our appreciation and expressions of thankfulness. There are many more if we are looking for them. See what small blessings God has planted in your life today. They make the trail more enjoyable.

Be sure to be thankful. Expressing gratefulness to God and others increases our joy and lets them share in the blessing.

~Wayne

~Further reading – 1 Chronicles 16:8-10, 29:12-13; Psalm 100; Matthew 6:28-30

ADVENTURE

Jeremiah 29:11 – *"For I know the plans that I have for you," declares the Lord, "plans for welfare and not for calamity to give you a future and a hope."*

Hiking has its adventures. "Adventure" is an event or action that involves danger or risk to the extent that it brings excitement, anxiety, and usually a response. For instance, there was the day Keith slipped on a wet boulder in the dangerous Mahoosic Notch, a maze of boulders in western Maine, and the deep spaces formed between the haphazard boulders.

Keith described that tense moment when he was hanging on by his fingers while looking down and not seeing a bottom. There was only blackness below him. Doubtless the surge of adrenaline in that intense moment gave him extra strength to pull himself to safety. His Mom and I had our own emotions when he described the event over the phone a couple days later.

Reaching a difficult-to-reach peak, coming across wild animals, facing intense weather events, enduring failed equipment, and encountering higher-than-expected rivers and narrow trails that drop off sharply on both sides all make for adventure. I found traversing a cascading creek on a narrow, thirty-foot log during a lightning storm in the 100 Mile Wilderness section of the AT in Maine to be a great adventure.

Walking life's trail with Jesus can be a great adventure. It becomes that when a Christian yields himself to Jesus to be the leader on the trail. God is at work building his kingdom, and he likes to include his adopted children in that work. Sometimes he has small tasks for us or even a restful day. But there are those days, weeks, or longer periods in which he gives us an adventurous assignment. Things like representing the Lord well in a hostile world, walking the narrow way in a world of immorality, sharing the gospel of Jesus with a lost person or persons, discipling a younger Christian, doing spiritual battle with a wounded friend, walking the difficult road with dying family members or close friends, serving on a short-term foreign missions team, and trusting God's promises when the "how to" is difficult to see, are some examples of adventures God gives us in doing his work.

Like those unexpected adventures along the hiking trails, Jesus does not always give us advance warning of an adventure he has planned for us (Eph. 2:10). However, he will always prepare us with his grace that is sufficient for our journey. Alice and I have both been through the cancer adventure—hers a bit more life-threatening than mine. She was not expecting the diagnosis her doctor gave her the morning we found out why she had been experiencing so much energy drain. That began a several-year, near-death adventure that resulted in her cure from cancer, growth in faith, and encouragement to several others with a testimony that glorifies God.

It is normal for us as human beings to see as bad the things that disrupt our lives, threaten us, or bring us pain. Yet the Christian is called to see these things through a different view, through the lens of Jesus' understanding. God has "good" in mind for us, so when "bad" things come into our lives, we can trust God to make good out of them in time.

Every day has the potential for adventure when walking in Jesus' plan for the day. Some adventures are an immediate blessing, such as having an opportunity to share with someone how to have a personal relationship with God or praying on the spot with someone expressing a need. I like to call these "divine appointments." Other adventures take place over long periods of time.

Try asking God at the beginning of your day to help you follow his leadership and to deal rightly with the adventures of the day. The Christian life is not for wimps. There is no more adventurous way to live than to walk in tune with the Lord.

~Wayne

~Further reading - Psalm 37; *The Life God Blesses* by Jim Cymbala

TAKE THE NEXT STEP

John 1:43 – *The next day He purposed to go into Galilee, and He found Philip. And Jesus said to him, "Follow Me."*

There is a group of men with whom I have joined for day hikes of eight to twelve miles. After hiking half the distance, usually to a particular point on the trail, we have lunch and relax a bit. The next step is to get up and take the first step on the hike back. My legs and spirit often rebel about that time and it takes will power and mind over matter to get my legs to move the way they need to go. It is amazing how each step after that seems to get easier for a while. I have noticed the other men usually have the same difficulty taking that first step.

A common saying is that a ship cannot be steered unless it is moving. I believe this is true of our lives. We do not make progress unless we are moving. I would have never made it through the 100 Mile Wilderness unless I had purposed and disciplined myself to take the first step each morning on that trail. There were times I would gladly have taken a ride back to camp if it had been available. Then again, I would have missed out on a tremendous memory that my son and I have of doing this special section of the AT together.

Keith would never have made it from Mount Katahdin to Springer Mountain if he had not purposed to take the first step on the AT from the top of Katahdin. He would not have even started if he had not purposed in his heart to hike the AT from end to end and to do the preparation necessary to be a successful through-hiker.

When Jesus prayed in the garden, "My Father, if it is possible, let this cup pass from me; yet not as I will, but as You will" (Matt. 26:39). He purposed at that point to take the next of many agony-laden steps toward Calvary to take our death penalty on the cross for our sin.

Perhaps God has impressed upon you the need for a more meaningful daily devotional time with the Lord. Then take the first step. Ask a friend to pray with you about it, find a time and place where you can get alone with God, put your Bible there, and get a devotional book to help you build the habit.

If you know that you need to break down a stronghold in your life, take the next step by giving it to the Lord in prayer and asking him to break it. Another step is to learn and meditate on scriptures that deal with your stronghold. I like to get an accountability partner or support group to help me through tough times.

Maybe you know that you need to share the hope of Jesus more often. Then ask God to help you recognize the opportunities to share your testimony and the gospel—the "divine appointments" I mentioned in the previous chapter. Practice with family and fellow church members if you need to grow more confident. Find someone who will go with you to visit.

Whatever you know you need to do, or whenever the Lord puts a step to take in your mind, take the next step right away, and then keep on taking the next step. Procrastination will steal your blessings of following in the steps of Jesus. If you start walking as God leads, you will one day look back and see that you have climbed a mountain, reached a goal, or are now helping someone else through troubles that no longer control you. It will bring joy in your life now and eternally. But, you must take the first and the next step!

~Wayne

~Further reading - 2 Timothy 2:15; Mathew 28:19-20; *Becoming a Contagious Witness* by Bill Hybels; *My Utmost for His Highest* by Oswald Chambers (a great book of devotions)

www.ingramcontent.com/pod-product-compliance
Lightning Source LLC
Chambersburg PA
CBHW021156080526
44588CB00008B/358